Volume 6, Issue 1 March 2002

Fashion and Photography

Special Issue

Edited by Carol Tulloch

Fashion Theory

The Journal of Dress, Body & Culture

Fashion Theory: The Journal of Dress, Body & Culture

Editor
Dr. Valerie Steele
The Museum at the Fashion Institute of Technology, E201
Seventh Avenue at 27th Street
New York, NY 10001-5992
USA
Fax: +1 212 924 3958
e-mail: steelemajor@earthlink.net

Book Reviews Editor
Christopher Breward
The London College of Fashion
20 John Princes Street
London W1M 0BJ

Exhibitions Reviews Editor
Bradley Quinn
27 Old Compton Street
London W1D 5JP

Please send all books for review to the Book Reviews Editor

Aims and Scope
The importance of studying the body as a site for the deployment of discourses is well-established in a number of disciplines. By contrast, the study of fashion has, until recently, suffered from a lack of critical analysis. Increasingly, however, scholars have recognized the cultural significance of self-fashioning, including not only clothing but also such body alterations as tattooing and piercing. *Fashion Theory* takes as its starting point a definition of 'fashion' as the cultural construction of the embodied identity. It aims to provide an interdisciplinary forum for the rigorous analysis of cultural phenomena ranging from footbinding to fashion advertising.

Anyone wishing to submit an article, interview, or a book, film or exhibition review for possible publication in this journal should contact Valerie Steele (at the address listed to the left) or the Editorial Department at Berg (150 Cowley Road, Oxford, OX4 1JJ, UK; e-mail: enquiry@berg.demon.co.uk).

Notes for Contributors can be found at the back of the journal.

ISSN: 1362-704X

Ordering Information Four issues per volume.   One volume per annum.   2002: Volume 6

By mail: Berg Publishers,
150 Cowley Road,
Oxford,
OX4 1JJ,
UK.

By fax: +44 (0) 1865 791165

By telephone: +44 (0) 1865 245104

By e-mail: enquiry@berg.demon.co.uk

Inquiries   Editorial: Kathryn Earle, Managing Editor, e-mail: kearle@berg1.demon.co.uk

Production: Sara Everett, e-mail: severett@berg.demon.co.uk

Advertising + subscriptions: enquiry@berg.demon.co.uk

Subscription Rates: Institutional base list subscription price: £89.00, US$145.00.   Individuals' subscription price: £35.00, US$55.00.

Reprints of Individual Articles   Copies of individual articles may be obtained from the Publishers at the appropriate fees. Write to: Berg, 150 Cowley Road, Oxford, OX4 1JJ, UK.   Printed in the United Kingdom. MARCH 2002

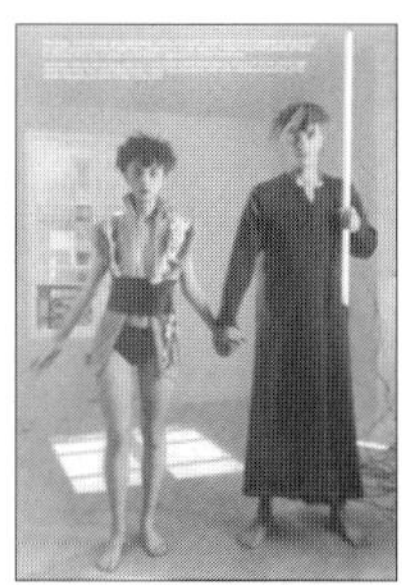

Page 3

Page 25

Page 45

Page 83

Page 111

Contents

Editor
Dr. Valerie Steele
The Museum at the Fashion
  Institute of Technology, E201
Seventh Avenue at 27th Street
New York, NY 10001-5992
USA

Fax +1 212 924 3958
e-mail: steelemajor@earthlink.net

Fashion Theory, Volume 6, Issue 1, pp. 1–2
Reprints available directly from the Publishers.
Photocopying permitted by licence only.
© 2002 Berg. Printed in the United Kingdom.

Letter from the Editor

The body of theoretical work on fashion photography is very small when compared with other areas of fashion theory such as gender or modernity. Most recent studies have generally concentrated on contemporary fashion photography and their creators. This issue goes some way to widening this. The publication was originally commissioned as a response to the Victoria and Albert Museum's exhibition *Imperfect Beauty: The Making of Contemporary Fashion Photography*, which Alistair O'Neill eloquently reviews here, and the complementary study day (October 2000) of the same name. The focus of the exhibition was to convey the behind-the-scenes production of the fashion image and the creative thought which inspire such productions. I was asked to organize the study day to tease out other facets and periods of the genre. The rationale I devised for that event works similarly for this special issue:

> The boundaries of what is acceptable on the pages of women's and men's fashion and style magazines have been consistently demolished since fashion photography's first tentative steps in the 1890s. More recently the producers of fashion images: photographers and stylists, models and make-up artists, graphic designers and art directors have all helped establish fashion photography as a legitimate, though often contentious, art form (*Imperfect Beauty: The Making of Contemporary Fashion Photography*, Study Day Leaflet, 2000).

The notion that the professional photographer is an impartial observer of life cannot be adhered to. The photographer, and this is equally relevant to the fashion photographer, makes an intervention into that milieu, and it is that intervention and their observations of daily events which fuel the photographer and the other members of a collaborative team to produce the fashion image they want. The articles featured here investigate this aspect of fashion photography to relate the other stories hidden behind the often glossy and perfect fashion images we see in magazines and posters, in advertisements or on billboards. They work on various levels with an underlying historical thread with case studies which stretch back to the 1930s. This is a refreshing aspect to the study of fashion photography in order to gain a better understanding of the continued power the practice has today. The essays demonstrate that fashion photography as a communicator of ideas and as a method of social commentary can work as a form of faction, incorporating real events as the basis for the creator's own brand of narrative. This is contentious as the auteur may well feel s/he is conveying some kind of truth. Nonetheless, within these endeavors, as demonstrated by Paul Jobling's scrutiny of new millennial narratives as signs of new beginnings and new technology as told through the fashion imagery of Andrea Giacobbe; and Paul Antick's study of the controversial Benetton advertising campaigns between 1983 and 1992.

The ubiquitous issue of identity suffuses these pages. Janice Cheddie and Rebecca Arnold base their work in the United States of America and reflect in their articles the weight of identity on different sections of its inhabitants, African- and white Americans, and how these identities are represented and read through fashion photography. Cheddie aims to eradicate the myth of why the black American model came to prominence in America in the early 1960s, while Arnold uses the fashion photographs of the American Louise Dahl-Wolfe to gain insight into what drives the American national identity. The possibilities for the fashion spread to go beyond being merely informative and to be a source of pleasure, to becoming an aid in the interior decoration of a home, and thereby to be viewed as another useful tool in the creation or extension of one's cultural identity is argued by Alice Beard. Through a combination of oral history, material and visual culture, Beard deliberates on the use made by consumers of fashion images from *Nova* magazine during its life from 1965 to 1975.

Fashion photography then is not just about slick images but comments on and contributes to life. We know that fashion photography is another form of communication, another form of story-telling, whether that be truth or fiction, nonetheless there is an attempt to make a point. What this package of five articles reiterates is that intellectual debate around fashion photography remains a necessary area of study and there is a need for a much larger body of work. I know in the main I am preaching to the converted, but there are dissenters out there, as Paul Jobling identifies, who think fashion photography is just about selling the accoutrements of dress through pretty pictures. Not so, there is so much more still to be said.

I would like to thank all the contributors for their hard work that has made this special edition possible, and to the staff at Berg for its production.

Carol Tulloch

Fashion Theory, Volume 6, Issue 1, pp. 3–24
Reprints available directly from the Publishers.
Photocopying permitted by licence only.

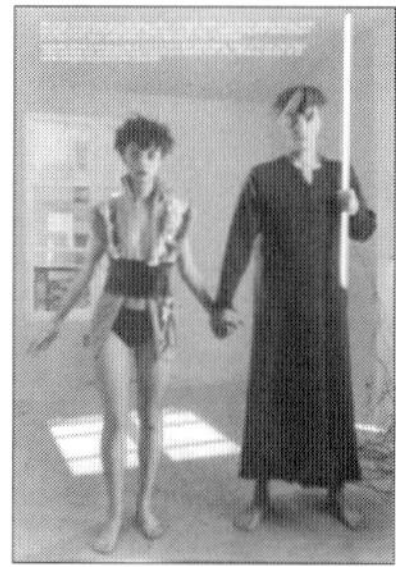

On the Turn— Millennial Bodies and The Meaning of Time in Andrea Giacobbe's Fashion Photography

Paul Jobling

Paul Jobling is a senior lecturer in the School of Historical and Critical Studies at the University of Brighton, UK. His recent publications include *Fashion Spreads—Word and Image in Fashion Photography Since 1980* (Berg, 1999). He is currently researching a book on advertising fashion and masculinities in Britain between 1920 and 1960.

A Millennial Prologue

In "Here Comes the Flood," one of the songs from The Divine Comedy's 1998 album *Fin de siècle*, vocalist Neil Hannon invokes rivers of mud, earthquakes, war, the arms-race and the space-race as symptoms of millennial angst and cataclysm, lamenting, "Here comes the blood bath . . . It's all over, we're all gonna die." This song encapsulates one of the long-held popular cultural mythologies concerning the turn of the century— the demise of civilization as we have come to know and understand it, and the concomitant downfall of mankind. At the close of the nineteenth century, for example, we find a similar consciousness expressed in a letter

published in the *Daily Chronicle* on 6 August 1895, in which the pseud-
onymous author "Unknown Quantity" inveighed: "Extravagance and
levity—a restless and morbid spirit—all that was implied by that tawdry,
borrowed, used-out, detestable word *fin de siècle*—these things have
brought us to the point of departure for revolution" (Stokes 1989: 7).
To be sure, sentiments like those expressed by "Unknown Quantity" and
The Divine Comedy can sound a bit overblown; yet they are also grounded
in cultural experience. The nemesis invoked by the former was informed
by the drift into godless bohemianism and debauchery and the constant
stimulation of the ego that critics such as Max Nordau had witnessed
taking place in urban culture since the 1880s.[1] While in our own time, a
whole cluster of concerns can be seen to have contributed to the troubling
chiliasm of The Divine Comedy track: the environmental disasters of
Chernobyl, global warming and the hole in the ozone layer; the trans-
global transmission of HIV and Aids through intravenous drug-taking
and unprotected sexual activity; the advent of BSE or mad cow disease
into the food chain; and ongoing civil warfare and ethnic tension in parts
of Europe, Africa and the Middle East.[2]

Of course, these concerns are not exclusively turn-of-the century or
millennial phenomena; but events such as death, disease and war
are thrown into sharper relief when time seems to be running out and
the imminent future appears uncertain. As Henry Porter has argued:
". . . many of us suspect that we are headed for some sort of collapse . . .
an ethical chaos inaugurated by the magic roundness of the year 2000"
(Porter 1995: 20). At the same time, there is always another, more optim-
istic side to things. For many people with socialist convictions during the
1890s, for instance, the turn of the century signaled death and decay in
a different sense, with the demise of the hegemonic class order implying
the dawn of a new, egalitarian age. Thus even "Unknown Quantity"
envisaged that many of the political and social upheavals of the 1890s
would lead not to downfall but to "a more healthy and manly spirit"
(Stokes 1989: 7). In France this kind of regenerative spirit was manifested
in the call to arms of the Cuban-born Marxist orator and writer Paul
Lafargue (1842–1911), who was imprisoned in 1891 for an incendiary
speech to a crowd of striking textile workers at Fourmies in the Nord, as
well as in paintings such as Paul Signac's "In Times of Harmony" (1893)
and lithographic images of liberation and atonement by left-wing graphic
artists, such as those of Maximilen Luce and Théophile Steinlen for the
radical periodical *Les Temps Nouveaux* (1895–1914).[3] During the late
1980s, a similar sense of social and political rebirth occurred in the
overthrowing of totalitarian Communist regimes in Poland, East Germany
and the Soviet Union, while the rise of the ecological movement and
G8 summits on environmental issues, such as that which resulted in
the Kyoto climate-change treaty in 1997, have sought to contest the
rampant consumerist ethos of capitalist societies and its impact on global
warming.[4]

But what, if anything, has such turn-of-the-century despair or optimism to do with fashion photography in the 1990s? Well, quite a lot, as it turns out. As Bethan Cole has argued, "End of the century mythology demands moral panic and fashion certainly seems to be providing it" (Cole 1997: 98). For instance, a recent spread photographed by Fabien Baron and styled by Karl Templer in the British fashion quarterly *Arena Homme Plus* (Autumn/Winter 1999) called "Techno Techno Techno, Clean Lines + Force 10 Fabrics," invokes the effects of global warming in its dramatic representation of water-drenched models heroically battling their way through a blasted, post-diluvian *mise-en-scène*. And one of the most salient themes to be explored in fashion photography from 1993 onwards is the involvement with drugs of both the fashion industry itself and youth culture at large, something that Rebecca Arnold has thoughtfully amplified in her article "Heroin Chic" in this journal in 1999.[5] At the same time, several other representations of millennial angst began to appear in fashion spreads in the early 1990s. "Meanwhile . . ." (*The Face*, February 1994) and "Global Warming TV" (*The Face*, September 1994), for example, both simulate the alienation and hollowness of late-twentieth-century consumer culture visited on the world by American corporatism. In contrast, "England's Dreaming" and "Head Hunters—Back to the no Future," both featured in *The Face* in August 1993, depict a discernible sense of anomic drift and youth rebellion in images of bohemian models either languidly lying about doing nothing or revisiting the anarchic dress codes of the Punk movement in an attempt to forge a contemporary identity.[6]

Indeed, one of the earliest indications of this turn-of-the-century imbrication of time and identity can be traced back to a fashion spread called "Veiled Threats," photographed by Andrew Macpherson and styled by Amanda Grieve, which appeared in *The Face* in January 1985. I have already discussed the historicist tropes of this spread and its mythological conflation of the late nineteenth and twentieth centuries in some detail in my book *Fashion Spreads*.[7] What I argued there was that the spread, with its admonition to "Do it your own way—progress on your terms—*fin de* nothing . . . keep it moving ahead," does not merely portray the turn of the century as a form of pessimistic closure, but also connotes a sense of transformative and redemptive time, that things do not ever really come to an end and past events can pave the way to a better (or at least a different) future. Accordingly, the relationship of the turn of the century to identity and the tension between traditional values and new beginnings are the key themes that I want to take the opportunity of elaborating in this article with specific reference to the work of Andrea Giacobbe, and in particular to the millennial symbolism of one of his fashion spreads, "Simplex Concordia," which appeared in *The Face* in July 1996 (Figures 1–3). On the one hand, I want to deal with the kinds of corporeal transubstantiation that take place in the spread in the context of cyborg theory, which, as the scientist Donna Haraway has cogently argued, "can suggest

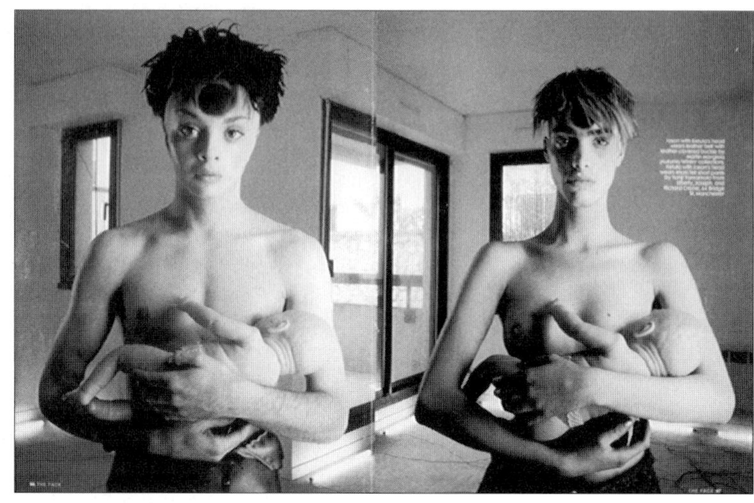

Figure 1
Andrea Giacobbe and Maida, "Simplex Concordia," Jason with Ketuta's head, Ketuta with Jason's head. Courtesy of *The Face*.

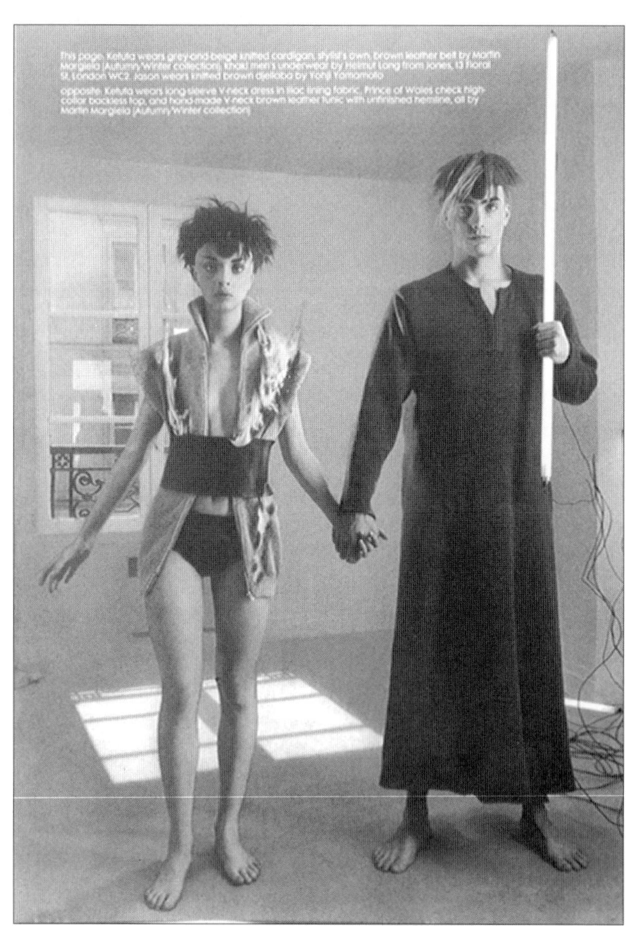

Figure 2
Andrea Giacobbe and Maida, "Simplex Concordia," Ketuta and Jason. Courtesy of *The Face*.

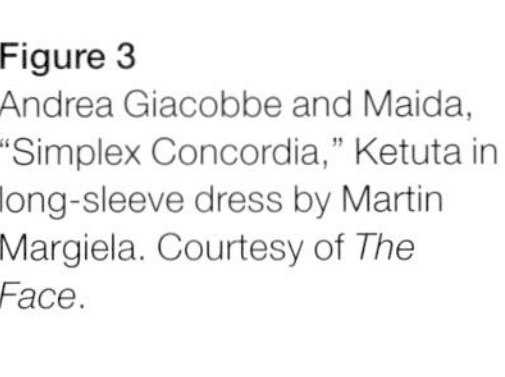

Figure 3
Andrea Giacobbe and Maida,
"Simplex Concordia," Ketuta in
long-sleeve dress by Martin
Margiela. Courtesy of *The
Face*.

a way out of the maze of dualisms in which we have explained our bodies and our tools to ourselves" (Haraway 1991: 181). And on the other, I want to account for its temporal symbolism in terms of *kairos* or apocalyptic time, which seems to offer, as the literary critic Frank Kermode contends, ". . . an escape from chronicity, and so, in some measure, a deviation from this norm of 'reality'" (Kermode 1966: 50). But first we need to account for the new technological forms of representation that have made such fictions possible.

Giacobbe and the Advent of Digital Photography: Technique and Style

Andrea Giacobbe was born in Florence in 1968. As an undergraduate in Italy he initially studied architecture, but after arriving in London sometime in 1987 he abandoned his program of studies in favor of photography. Between 1987 and 1988 he worked as a studio assistant to Paolo Roversi and Andrew Macpherson, whose work had been published in *Vogue* and *Arena* respectively, and at the same time he began to photograph the collections of the Japanese designer Atsuro Tayama.[8]

Eventually he attended the Arts Institute at Bournemouth, taking a diploma course in creative photography between 1989 and 1992,[9] and after graduating he relocated to Paris to begin his career as an independent professional photographer. He soon found work for the cult Paris publication, *Citizen K*, and his photographs also appeared in *The Face* for the first time in the autumn of 1994. In collaboration with the stylist Maida, he produced four spreads for *The Face* between 1994 and 1996: "Leisure Lounge" (October 1994), "ark life" (March 1995), "littleearth" (February 1996) and "Simplex Concordia" (July 1996). Along with more recent work for *Dazed and Confused* such as "La Comédie 2000" (December/January 2000), and his video productions for bands like Garbage in 1998,[10] Giacobbe's imagery tends to be electronically mediated, and demonstrates a clear technical and aesthetic reliance on computer artwork applications such as Quantel Paintbox, Barco and Adobe Photoshop.[11]

One of the most significant developments in allying digital technology to photography, however, can be traced back to the debut of the electronic non-film still camera in 1982. This functioned more or less like a conventional 35mm handheld camera, but relied on a charge-coupled device (CCD) as the imaging sensor. In contrast to analog forms of photography, which involve the chemical processing of negative film to positive print, the CCD recorded the image on a disk as a grid of digitized pixels and eliminated any need for developing from negative to positive in the darkroom; now the image could be transmitted directly on to a video screen and its pixels edited accordingly.[12] By 1987, electronic transmitters also made the movement of images from digital cameras to computers more reliable, and resulted in higher-density resolution.[13] Initially, these electronically-generated images were the province of photojournalism, with its tight deadlines and demands for immediacy. But the advent of the Apple Macintosh computer in 1984, in conjunction with programs such as Quark Xpress, Paintbox and Photoshop, also facilitated more creative forms of multi-media digital editing involving the manipulation not just of still images but of video and film as well. Along with flatbed photographic scanners, these image-manipulation programs began to be more cheaply and widely marketed by the mid-1990s, and as a result photographers, film-makers and video artists could download them on to their own personal computers rather than relying totally on specialist digital labs to process their simulated images for them.[14] As the photographer Victor Burgin attests, the potential for creative freedom and synergy that the new multimedia packages offered was almost infinite:

> . . . you can take a video-tape or a laser disc of film, and you can send the signal to the computer and watch the film on the screen. You can stop it, reverse it, put it in slow motion, and so on. And you can behave like a photographer in the street. You can grab that Cartier-Bresson-inspired moment, and save it . . . The computer

gives you the power to shift everything around in the film. I can take a character from one scene, store the character in the attitude that I've selected, and then I can move that character into any of the other scenes (Burgin 1991: 8).

Yet not all image-makers have demonstrated unequivocal support for the advent and wholesale adoption of digital photography. Dunstan Perera, the inventor of the Heliochrome photography printing process, for example, impugned the sense of economic and artistic division that seem to have attended the new technologies, insisting: "If the current trend continues, photography as we know it will only be practised by two groups: amateurs and photographers in third world countries, where they cannot afford digital technology" (Perera 2000: 43). While viewing the majority of images produced with the aid of computers as sterile and lacking in personal style, at the same time he does concede that "in the hands of a talented photographer they can be an asset" (2000: 43). This idea of individuality is very much the concern of Giacobbe who, when asked about his fashion spread "La Comédie," published in the December/ January 2000 issue of *Dazed and Confused*, responded gnomically, "I wanted to create images that were purely subjective" (Flett 2000: 23).

Such acts of digitized simulation, however, were to become just one stylistic option in the repertoire of fashion photographers working after 1988. In a review of the recent exhibition, "Imperfect Beauty: The Making of Contemporary Fashion Photographs," which was held at the Victoria and Albert Museum in London, Ekow Eshun identifies two prevalent camps in contemporary fashion photography: the Romantic Realists— photographers like Corinne Day and Juergen Teller, whose images are still analog-based and whose subjects are photographed in actual rather than constructed environments; and the Master Manipulators—photographers like Elaine Constantine and Giacobbe, whose digitized images with their simulated environments mimic the appearance of reality (Eshun 2000: 25).[15] But of course, this dichotomy does not mean that analog photographs are necessarily more authentic or truthful than digital ones for, as Eshun also testifies, the Romantic Realists "sought to capture, not outward glamour, but inner radiance." In each of these stylistic camps, therefore, the gulf between fantasy or imagination and realism is not always so clear-cut, and what seems to matter more is the way that photographs can resonate with cultural meanings according to the way they are presented to us and the way that we frame them as individuals. Thus Andy Cameron argues: "Photographs are not simply believed because they are photographs—we assess them as we assess all propositions—according to what we want to believe, what we already believe, what we believe is likely, and above all, according to the channels of authority through which they circulate" (*TEN.8* 1991: 4–5).

Although such computer-manipulated images appear to transcend any straightforward sense of reality, therefore, the intention of many digital photographers is not merely a matter of escapism but rather of contextualization, and Vincent Peters has argued that the point of such digitization is "how you bring fashion and reality together" (Flett 2000:20). Accordingly, in common with the use of photomontage by the likes of Hannah Höch and John Heartfield in the 1920s and 1930s, the new technologies afford the Master Manipulators an opportunity to reconfigure images and conjure up strange new worlds that will invite spectators to ruminate on the meaning of their own worldly existence in more complex ways.[16] Where the traditional photomontagist relied literally on cutting and pasting together fragments of analog photographs with glue and scissors, however, now the digital photographer cuts and pastes electronically, altering his/her compositions through the matrix of pixellated cells held in the computer database. Moreover, unlike analog or film-based images, the electronic image does not leave any trace of the manipulations performed on it.

Forging a Futuristic Content

Fashion photography thus began to be transformed exponentially by the use of computer technologies during the late 1980s. But this was not merely a question of changing style or technique for its own sake; rather it involved taking an inventive approach to content as well. As the critics Steve Bode and Paul Wombell (Wombell 1991: 6) and William J. Mitchell attest, "the sudden crystallization of a new technology . . . provides the nucleus for new forms of social and cultural practice and marks the beginning of a new era of artistic exploration" (Mitchell 1992: 20). Now it was possible to escape the studio and eschew shooting on location, and to construct imaginative narrative tableaux by recombining models and backdrops on the computer screen with the help of Paintbox and Photoshop.

One of the first fashion photographers to work in this way was Stephane Sednaoui.[17] In collaboration with the art director Elisabeth Djian he spent two months producing a prolonged photo shoot called "Showdown—The Battle for Planet Fashion" for the October 1989 issue of *The Face*. Across twenty-four pages Sednaoui and Djian elaborated a science fiction spoof in words and images that depicted the struggle of Fashion sometime in the distant future to rid the world of Conformity, represented in the form of a diabolic figure. In the ensuing strife between the forces of light and darkness, planet Fashion saves the day with the aid of the designers Vivienne Westwood, Jean Paul Gaultier, Azzedine Alaïa, Martine Sitbon and Thierry Mugler, and Conformity is consigned back to planet Jealousy. This narrative seems little more than a deliberate exercise in kitsch, but the images themselves are highly creative and flaunt their electronic status in the use of special effects and dayglo colors. Particularly striking are the scenes that transmute the bodies of two of the models into Cyclone Woman and Ant Woman respectively, as well as a photograph of the five fashion designers themselves, who have been surrounded by luminous electric haloes and dropped into a scorched red background complete with air bubbles.[18] Moreover, the apocalyptic theme of the spread and its vision of a future and a place where identities are transformative and time is redemptive, seems to pave the way for the millennial messages contained in the four fashion spreads photographed by Andrea Giacobbe and styled by Maida for *The Face* between 1994 and 1996. But whereas the futuristic *topos* of Sednaoui's narrative unequivocally occupies outer space, Giacobbe's millennial vision unfolds in terrestrial landscapes and milieux.

"littleearth" (*The Face*, February 1996) for example, has been shot in California and represents four new-age characters—a Red Indian chief, a little white girl, and two young ethnic women. They wear various garments in synthetic fabrics designed by Walter Van Beirendonck for his W< label, and have literally been dropped into the various terrains they each inhabit. The general message of the spread seems to deal with the harnessing of tradition to new technologies, connoted both by the different types of models and the garments worn, and the juxtaposition of nature with objects like windmills and solar reactors, as well as in the captions—"We can't go backwards. Every age has its own practical problems." The male and female models in the remaining three shoots by Giacobbe and Maida likewise occupy recognizable spaces—a nightclub ("Leisure Lounge," *The Face*, October 1994), fields and motorways ("ark life," *The Face*, March 1995), and an apartment ("Simplex Concordia," *The Face*, July 1996). In each of these spreads, however, the models are much more other-worldly in appearance and seem to be matter out of place—their faces shine with metallic make-up and they perform unsettling or disorienting acts. In one of the images from "Leisure Lounge," we observe the model in the process of replacing one of her eyeballs (Figure 4), while in "ark life" a man sits in a car with a rooster on his lap. But the alien identities and the strange acts they perform in each of these instances have probably been represented in more extreme terms in "Simplex Concordia," although the woolen, cotton and leather garments by Paul Smith, Martin Margiela and Yohji Yamamoto that are worn by the two models are not necessarily alien or futuristic in terms of cut and materials.[19] In fact, in several images either clothing is absent altogether or else it is marginal to the ostensible narrative that is elaborated in the spread.

In the first opening of the piece we encounter a picture on the left, which is tinted green and depicts a narcissus in a plastic bottle on a table alongside a tumbler half-filled with yellow liquid. In the background are a set of empty bookshelves, a green dining chair and a light-table. The facing picture on the right represents the two models Jason and Ketuta in a spartan living room, which is tinted red and illuminated by fluorescent lights. They appear to be wearing distressed wigs over their shaved heads

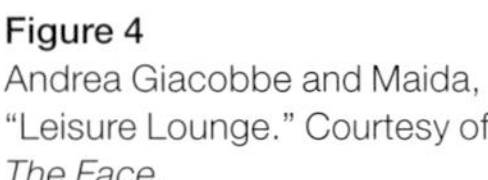

Figure 4
Andrea Giacobbe and Maida,
"Leisure Lounge." Courtesy of
The Face.

and, kneeling face-to-face on the floor with their groins pressed together, they project their reptile-like tongues at each other as if involved in some strange mating ritual. When we turn the page we see them kneeling again and dipping some undergarments into a bowl that is filled with green liquid and placed in front of them on the floor. This time they face us and we can also make out that they both have a black disk emblazoned on the middle of their foreheads. Adjacent to this image is a picture of Ketuta, naked but for a pair of men's underpants, standing in a bath filled with the same green liquid, with which she has also anointed her skin.[20] What follows is a half-length photograph of the naked couple, who gaze directly out at us as they stand side by side in the bay window of a red-tinted room. This image seems to form a pendant with the next opening, which depicts Jason with Ketuta's head and Ketuta with Jason's head

(Figure 1). Here the gaze and stance of the couple are similar to those in the previous photograph, but they are located in a green room and, having apparently changed gender, they each nestle a baby to their breast. In turn, the final two pictures form a marked contrast (Figures 2 and 3). In the first, Jason and Ketuta stand holding hands in a magenta room; she is wearing a knitted cardigan and brown leather corsage by Martin Margiela, which have been set on fire, and he is wearing a long-sleeve knitted V-neck djellaba by Yohji Yamamoto and, warrior-like, holds a fluorescent lamp erect in his left hand. In the last image, we observe Ketuta standing alone in the kitchen. She has dropped a glass of milk on the floor and she tramples on it, with blood dripping from her bare feet. As she does so, once more she gazes out at us, and we notice now that she has different-colored eyes—her right one is green, and her left brown (as it is in the other photographs).

As we turn the pages of the spread each of the photographs has its own momentum and there does not appear to be any strict sense of denouement taking place. On the surface, therefore, "Simplex Concordia" presents us with a structural *aporia*, and functions on the level of the postmodernist anti-narrative that tends, as Robert Scholes aptly puts it, "to problematize the entire process of narration and interpretation for us" (Scholes 1980: 211). Although we may initially find the tropes of the spread inchoate or incohesive, nonetheless its authors exhort us to try to interpret or decode it. The tagline on the opening page states, "End of the millennium paranoia seeks spiritual salvation. All reasonable offers considered." Taking up this hermeneutic challenge, then, I would suggest that there are two significant, interrelated ways in which we can cognitively frame "Simplex Concordia" with regard to its latent millennial symbolism—first, by analyzing its depiction of fluid human identities; and second, by considering the way that it seems to deal with future time in terms of apocalyptic degeneration versus redemption: "It is not just the making and remaking of bodies, but the making and remaking of worlds which is crucial here" (Featherstone and Burrows 1995: 2).

Loving the Alien: Replication and Reproduction

In the spread the world appears to have been turned upside down and Jason and Ketuta do not always appear to understand how to make sense of the dystopian spaces they inhabit; they wash their clothing and bodies in what passes for undiluted detergent, for instance. Ketuta also wears a cardigan that is ablaze and stands in a puddle of spilt milk, her feet bloodied from the broken glass, ostensibly without feeling any pain. Furthermore, in all the photographs their poses are wooden and somewhat cataleptic, and although they look out at us their gaze seems impenetrable. This sense of alienation is compounded by the black spots that stigmatize their foreheads, and is particularly heightened in the opening, where they cross genders but can still both breastfeed. Quite clearly then, Giacobbe, who is an avid follower of science fiction, has not represented mere earthlings or "pure" human beings in this spread, but bodies that are insensible to heat and discomfort and can mutate into the opposite sex.[21] In other words, what we seem to be dealing with here is a form of cyborg culture, although not one that unmistakably portrays the cybernetic organism as part-human, part-machine.[22] Rather, Giacobbe seems to mimic the idea of the human replicant portrayed in Philip K. Dick's novel *Do Androids Dream of Electric Sheep?* (1968). Inhabiting Los Angeles in the year 2019, this replicant is a being that suffers injury without feeling it and is able to repair itself spontaneously, unlike its flesh and blood counterpart. In *Blade Runner* (1982), Ridley Scott's film adaptation of the novel, the most advanced of these replicants, such as Rachel, are also devoid of memory and have been programmed so that not only do they fail to recognize themselves as replicants but they are notoriously difficult for the untutored eye to identify as well—hence the role of blade runners like Deckard, who is a member of a special police force trained to unmask and tame them.[23] Yet in the narratives of both Dick and Scott, the replicants are slaves deployed in the Tyrell Corporation's extra-terrestrial colonies, whereas in "Simplex Concordia" they are represented much more as autonomous beings, and as such they seem to be what Donna Haraway has called creatures of "social reality . . . as well as . . . of fiction," who inhabit a "post-gender world" (Haraway 1991: 149 and 150).

In "A Cyborg Manifesto" Haraway writes: "My cyborg myth is about transgressed boundaries, potent fusions, and dangerous possibilities which progressive people might explore as one part of needed political work" (1991: 154). What is particularly at stake during the late twentieth century, she argues, is the disruption or blurring of normative concepts concerning identities, be they sexual, racial or class-based:

> I do not know of any other time in history when there was greater need for political unity to confront effectively the dominations of "race," "gender," "sexuality," and "class" . . . None of "us" have any longer the symbolic or material capability of dictating the shape of reality to any of "them." Or at least "we" cannot claim innocence from practising such dominations (1991: 157).

Thus in Haraway's epistemology the cyborg is quintessentially disruptive and subversive, resisting the "dream of community" and defining "a technological polis based partly on a revolution of social relations in the *oikos*, the household" (1991: 151). This reframing of household relations seems to be exactly what is taking place in "Simplex Concordia." Not only is the home invaded by replicants who behave dysfunctionally within it, but the role of female as natural housekeeper and childbearer has been breached. In the spread home is connoted as a fundamentally messy place, and Figure 1 plays on the tension between what Elizabeth Potter has called *hic mulier/haec vir* (masculine woman/feminine man) (Haraway 1997: 29–32). Thus Ketuta and Jason are depicted as transgendered breast-feeders, which implies that now both male and female subjects have the ability to reproduce: "Sex, sexuality, and reproduction are central actors in high-tech myth systems structuring our imaginations of personal and social possibility" (Haraway 1991: 169). Moreover, the representation of Jason as a maternal figure in this photograph appears to transcend the "womb envy" that Mary Ann Doane identifies as one of the chief themes of cyborg films like *Terminator* (1984), in which the male protagonist desires to be the generator of human life (Doane 1990: 169).

It is cyborg theories by Haraway and others, therefore, with their emphasis on utopian and transformative identities, that probably illuminate the symbolism of millennial bodies like Jason and Ketuta in "Simplex Concordia" to best effect. But both cyborg culture as Haraway analyzes it and Giacobbe's fashion spread do not merely portend a mythological vision of what may come to pass in the future, they resonate the hopes and fears of what is already possible at the dawning of the second millennium with the widespread use of new technologies and genetic engineering. Haraway propounds: "Communications technologies and biotechnologies are the crucial tools recrafting our bodies" (1991: 164). Thus, on the one hand, the rise of digitized systems of information has facilitated the representation of more cogent hybrid identities, while on the other, gender reassignment and cloning have literally enabled the transcendence of our biological bodies and destinies. Biomedical methods of assisted reproduction have already led to the modification of DNA, the molecule that carries the blueprint for life itself, in the fertilized eggs of mammals. In experiments by Ian Wilmut and Keith Campbell, for example, this resulted notoriously in the production of Dolly, a lamb whose genetic make-up was cloned from the udder of a dead ewe (Silver 1998), while Peter Goodfellow and Robin Lovell-Badge successfully transformed female embryos into male ones by injecting the Sry gene into the fertilized eggs of mice (Wilkie 1991). There is currently an international moratorium on similar forms of cloning and genetic mutation in human beings, witness the Human Fertilization and Embryology Act (1990) in England and Wales. Nonetheless, such scientific experimentation and the founding of the Human Genome Diversity Project in 1991 to collect genetic tissue from over 700 groups of indigenous peoples across the world have opened up the potential for biotechnological engineering and *ex utero* forms of gestation that are adumbrated by the transgendered creatures in feminist science fiction such as Joanna Russ's *The Female Man* and James Tiptree Jr's *Star Songs of an Old Primate* (Haraway 1991: 247, 1997: 69–78), and indeed by Jason and Ketuta.[24] It is not for nothing, after all, that Giacobbe's fashion spread bears the title "Simplex Concordia," to allude to the potential of the simplex cell not only to replicate but also to transform itself genetically.

The Replicant and Redemptive Time

But the significance of these transmutations takes on additional weight in the context of the millennium and, to paraphrase Constance Penley (1990: 119), the symbolic content of "Simplex Concordia" (as well as of the other fashion spreads addressed in this article) bears on the relationship of identities to time. As we have already seen, in the penultimate photograph of the sequence Jason and Ketuta are represented as warriors, clasping hands while she goes up in flames like some latter-day Brünnhilde and he holds up a fluorescent striplight/magic wand as if in homage to Luke Skywalker (Figure 2). The image, therefore, seems to inaugurate the millennial "spiritual salvation" that the opening tagline enjoins us to seek, by harping on the idea of the Twilight of the Gods, a sacrificial event by which mankind will be redeemed. In this sense, then, the fictional time of the spread seems to represent the distinction that Frank Kermode (1966) elicits between *chronos*, or passing time, the succession of one moment by another, which he likens to the *tick-tick* of a clock, and *kairos*, or seasonal time, which he likens to *tick-tock* since it is special or commemorative and implies a sense of closure. As Kermode puts it, *kairos* is "poised between beginning and end . . . a point in time filled with significance, charged with meaning derived from its relation to the end" (1966: 46, 47). In other words it is "time-redeeming" time (1966: 52), which is symbolized in the penultimate image of "Simplex Concordia" by the way Jason and Ketuta appear to have struck a covenant that sediments the new social and sexual order connoted in those preceding it.

And yet, on the surface, the fashion spread ends on a disquieting note and portrays a sense of crisis, for the final photograph of Ketuta wearing a long-sleeve lilac dress and brown tunic by Martin Margiela standing on her own in the kitchen (Figure 3) returns us once more to a world turned upside-down. The presence of blood and the absence of Jason lead us to ponder on this as a scene of altercation and perhaps even of murder. In this respect it is tempting to regard Ketuta as the archetypal castrating, female double that Freud raises in his 1919 essay "The Uncanny." In this, he recounts Hoffman's story of "The Sand-Man," in which Professor Spalanzani has invented Olympia, a fantastic living automaton. In due course, a young student called Nathaniel falls in love with her; but this induces his downfall, sending him into a state of madness in which he begins to confuse reality and fantasy. Thus, when he observes the doll without any eyes, it awakens in him a fear born in childhood of losing his own eyesight to "The Sand-Man," a mythological character whom his mother used to invoke in order to get her children to go to bed early. This brings Freud to extrapolate that Olympia, the "double" that Nathaniel first took to be a benign figure that could ward off the threat of blindness (and, by extension, castration), ultimately becomes the "uncanny harbinger of death" (Freud 1985: 356–7). Consequently, the closing image begs the question: what is the price, or indeed even the point, of sexual transformation and liberation if it leads to death and destruction?

Far from simply being a castrating double-dealer, however, we must remember that Ketuta belongs to a post-Oedipal, cyborg world that has subverted the idea of penis-envy (if not castration anxiety) by enabling men and women to have gender reassignment and prosthetic surgery. As Haraway insists, "The cyborg is a creature in a post-gender world" (1991: 151). In which case, the last photograph of the sequence appears to revolve around a double-take that invites us to consider the meaning of *kairos* on another level.

Julia Kristeva argues that confrontation with certain foodstuffs, such as milk, leads to an extreme form of abjection or convulsive behavior that brings identity to a crisis by disavowing any link with the Oedipal order of things: ". . . that milk cream separates me from the mother and father who proffer it. 'I' want none of that element, sign of their desire" (1982: 3). Certainly, in the way that Ketuta treads in the spilt milk and the blood pours from her feet there seems to be a similar kind of reckoning with body fluids taking place. Figure 1, for example, already connotes that both she and Jason have transcended any straightforward biological relationship with milk. Accordingly, in Figure 3 the bloodstains on her feet seem to signify not just decadence and downfall but also revolution and retribution, and she bears them like the stigmata of the risen Christ as if to proclaim that not "man," but "woman" will be the Messiah of the new millennium—a point that takes *fin-de-siècle* images of female liberators by graphic artists like Steinlen, which I mentioned in my introduction, to a more transgressive millennial conclusion. Thus Figure 3 transforms the New Testament idea of *kairos* as the coming of God's time, or the fulfilling of time, to mean the epiphany of woman's time, and in such a way as to remind me of another nineteenth-century antecedent— the typological representations of female Biblical characters by Julia Margaret Cameron.[25]

In works such as *Contributions to the Literature of the Fine Arts* (1848), writers such as Sir Charles Eastlake had maintained that the aim of typology was to reveal the correspondences between Old Testament and New Testament subjects by portraying the former as prefigurements of the latter (Weaver 1984: 20), and this is what Cameron also set out to achieve in her photographs. With "The Return After Three Days" (1865), for example, she appeared to fuse together the Old Testament story of the return of the dove to Noah's ark after the great flood with the return of Christ after his crucifixion in the New Testament. But, influenced by Anna Jameson, she also tended to represent female or androgynous characters—in this instance the daughters of Noah or the three Marys— to symbolize that women rather than men were present to witness the rebirth of the world and of time. Hence Mike Weaver suggests: "The possibilities of a theological feminism were not lost on Cameron" (Weaver 1984: 23).

Kermode has contended that the transformative potential of typological forms of representation has been an ongoing process since the nineteenth century, arguing: "We seek to repeat the performance of the New Testament, a book which rewrites and requites another book and achieves harmony with it rather than questioning its truth" (1966: 59). Far from echoing this harmony, however, or simply being a "fiction of concord" (ibid.), "Simplex Concordia" seems to mobilize typology for more subversive ends (as Cameron had before Giacobbe) to portend a future that takes an unexpected turn by putting polymorphous male and female replicants at centre stage:

> Cyborg writing must not be about the Fall, the imagination of a once-upon-a-time wholeness before language, before writing, before Man. Cyborg writing is about the power to survive, not on the basis of the original innocence, but on the basis of seizing the tools to mark the world that marked them as other (Haraway 1991: 175).

Conclusion

This exploration of the symbolism of millennial bodies and apocalyptic time in fashion spreads has taken us quite a long way, and in concluding it, I am consciously attuned to the plaintive cry raised by some students in seminar discussions—"It's only a fashion photograph. Aren't you taking things a bit too far?" Well, not necessarily, and readers of my earlier work on fashion photography will not be surprised to hear me reiterate Susan Sontag's point at this stage of my discussion that "fashion photography is much more than the photography of fashion" (Sontag 1978: 104). After all, Giacobbe and *The Face* themselves seem only too well aware of the hermeneutic games they are playing with us by postulating at the outset of "Simplex Concordia" that "End of millennium paranoia seeks spiritual salvation. All reasonable offers considered." On this level, the spread trades on a traditional sense of apocalyptic anxiety and crisis that can be traced back to Antiquity.[26] Writers as early as Plato seem to have appreciated that, as time advances, an unsettling sense of dissolution and reorientation is inevitable. Yet nor does this have to be an entirely negative thing—in the last stages of democratic civilization, for example, which Plato envisages in *The Republic* as an age of mixed metal following on from those of gold, silver, bronze and iron, all hierarchies are dissolved and there is no longer any distinction between the sexes or between citizens and foreigners (Plato 1974: 361–2). This is precisely the scenario that seems to be represented in the cyborg narrative of "Simplex Concordia," so that although it appears to connote a world order that is still to come it also opens our eyes to the admonition of both Plato and Haraway that transformative, if not redemptive, time is never as far away as we imagine: "We require regeneration, not rebirth, and the possibilities for our reconstitution include the utopian dream of the hope for a monstrous world without gender" (Haraway 1991: 181).

Notes

1. Max Nordau's massive work *Degeneration* is probably the most sustained, contemporaneous exploration of the *fin-de-siècle* malaise. In it, for example, he observes: "In our days there have arisen in more highly developed minds vague qualms of a Dusk of Nations, in which all suns and stars are gradually waning, and mankind with all its institutions and creations is perishing in the midst of a dying world . . . The disposition of the times is currently confused, a compound of feverish restlessness and blunted discouragement, of fearful presage and hangdog renunciation. The prevalent feeling is that of imminent perdition and extinction" (Nordau 1895: 1 and 2). In this regard, he particularly excoriates the philosopher Friedrich Nietzsche, who had formulated his doctrine of Dionysian hedonism in works such as *Beyond Good and Evil* (1886) and *The Will to Power* (1887–8), in Book III, Chapter V of *Degeneration*. The following comment gives a flavor of Nordau's opposition: "From the first to the last page of Nietzsche's writings the careful reader seems to hear a madman, with flashing eyes, wild gestures, and foaming mouth, spouting forth deafening bombast; and through it all, now breaking out into frenzied laughter, now sputtering expressions of filthy abuse and invective, now skipping about it in a giddily agile dance, and now bursting upon the auditors with threatening mien and clenched fists. So far as any meaning at all can be extracted from the endless stream of phrases, it shows, as its fundamental elements, a series of constantly reiterated delirious ideas, having their source in illusions of sense and diseased organic processes . . ." (1895: 416).
2. See the following authors for various perspectives on these issues and their relationship to millennial angst: Halliday (2001); Jay and Neve (1999); Porter (1995); and Showalter (1991).
3. See the following texts for a wider assessment of turn-of-the-century socialism and anarchism in France: L. Derfler, *Paul Lafargue and the Flowering of French Socialism, 1882–1911*, Boston, MA: Harvard University Press, 1998; E. Dixmier and M. Dixmier, *"L'Assiette au beurre" revue satirique illustrée*, Paris: Maspero, 1974; S. Gill, "Steinlen's Prints: Social Imagery in Late 19th-Century Graphic Art," *Print Collector's Newsletter*, Vol. X, No. 1, March/April 1979.
4. The University of Toronto, G8 Centre website (http://www.library. utoronto.ca) is a mine of information on these matters. See, for example, Dan Esty, "A Global Environment Organization: The Fourth Bretton Woods Pillar."

5. I also included some assessment of heroin chic in my analysis of Corinne Day's "Under Exposure" (British *Vogue*, June 1993), which featured Kate Moss disporting herself at home in various states of undress. See Jobling (1999), Chapter 6, pp. 111–18.

6. David Lachapelle and Arianne Phillips, "Meanwhile . . .," *The Face*, February 1994: 52–9; Inez Van Lamsweerde and Vinoodh Matadin, "Global Warming TV," *The Face*, September 1994: 130–40; Corinne Day and Melanie Ward, "England's Dreaming," and Jean Baptiste Mondino and Judy Blame, "Head Hunters—Back to No Future," *The Face*, August 1993, pp. 80–9 and 104–13. See also the following fashion spreads in *The Face*; Jean Baptiste Mondino and Maida, "Full Metal Jacket" (September 1994, pp. 66–73); Schoerner and Nancy Rohde, "Quest for Albion" (January 1995, pp. 100–11); David Lachapelle and Arianne Phillips, "The New Seekers" (April 1995, pp. 116–25); Schoerner and Adam Howe, "Planet Waves" (August 1996, pp. 128–35); Schoerner and Joanne Yi, "Sunspots" (November 1996, pp. 162–71).

7. Jobling (1999), pp. 42–5, 59–62.

8. Tayama had started out as a fashion assistant to Yohji Yamamoto between 1977 and 1982, before launching his own label. He is currently the driving force behind five fashion labels—Atsuro Tayama, AT, OZOC, Boycott, and Indivi. Frances La Gavin (1999), pp. 42–3, described his clothing as "Unrestricted clothing for open minds."

9. Between 1990 and 1992 Wolfgang Tillmans also attended The Arts Institute Bournemouth (formerly Bournemouth and Poole College of Art and Design). After graduating Tillmans worked for *i.D* (1989–1997) and *The Face* (1990), although, like Giacobbe, he has not ever regarded himself exclusively as a fashion photographer. In 2000 he was the winner of the Turner Prize. See Riemschneider (1995) and Tillmans (1998).

10. Giacobbe directed the video for Garbage's track "Push It" in April 1998, which was nominated for eight MTV independent music awards, including best director. His videography also includes "Dirt" for Death in Vegas (September 1997), and "Revolution Action" for Atari Teenage Riot (July 1999). The latter was banned by MTV in Europe because of its controversial visual effects, which represent the tearing off of a kidnapped businessman's face.

11. As the credits for some fashion spreads remind us, it must also be borne in mind that both fashion photographer and stylist rely on a number of other technicians and specialists to help them carry their ideas to fruition. "Simplex Concordia," for example, also involved photographic assistance from Stephane Milone and Andrea Newell, electronic retouching by Janvier, and help with special effects by Gwendolyne (*The Face*, July 1996, p. 99).

12. A digitally produced photograph is made up of a series of small picture cells—pixels—each of which is number-coded by the computer according to the brightness of a gray scale or the three primary colors. After a chemical or analog photograph has been logged or scanned into a computer, it is broken down into a grid of pixels in the same manner.

13. The qualitative and ethical impact of the idea of electronic spontaneity on photojournalism was widely assessed in the American professional journal *News Photographer* during the 1980s. See K. E. Becker, "To Control Our Image: Photojournalists Meeting New Technology" (Wombell 1991: 16–30) for an informed and interesting account of these debates.

14. When first introduced in 1984, Quantel Paintbox, for example, retailed at a prohibitive £80,000.

15. The exhibition was curated by Charlotte Cotton, assistant curator of photographs, and displayed in the Canon Photography Gallery between 28 September 2000 and 18 March 2001. It focused on the contribution of the stylist as much as the photographer in the evolution of photographic images. A complementary book was also published: see Cotton (2000).

16. Lavin (1993), for example, is a penetrating study of how Hannah Höch used photomontage during the Weimar Republic (1919–32) to explore the role of female identities in patriarchal society.

17. Sednaoui started his fashion career as a catwalk model for Jean Paul Gaultier in 1983 before moving into photography. He was also casting director for William Klein's movie *Mode in France* (1985), which was commissioned by the French Ministry of Culture to showcase the work of designers like Gaultier and Azzedine Alaïa. Now living in Manhattan, like Giacobbe he works mostly in music video production. He won an MTV award for his direction of "Give It Away" for the Red Hot Chili Peppers, and his credits also include "Fever" for Madonna, "Big Time Sensuality" for Björk, and "She Moves in Mysterious Ways" for U2.

18. In an interview with Cotton (2000), pp. 100–1, Sednaoui seems to compress this chronology, implying that he worked for *The Face* in 1989 only (in fact, his earliest contribution to the magazine, "Voici Paris," had been published in June 1988). He also seems to negate the fact that during 1989 he was relying on digital technologies as well as photomontage. Thus he avows, "I actually didn't use any machines—it was all done by hand," whereas *The Face* (October 1989), p. 3, states quite plainly, that "Stephane spent weeks manipulating the images by computer . . .".

19. Futuristic, cyborg-related developments in fashion by 1996 included the integration of electronic devices, such as the garment designs pioneered by Massachussetts Institute of Technology (Kelly 1994) and Nancy Tilbury for Philips (Roberts 1999: 17). In textiles,

meanwhile, considerable advance had been made in combining synthetic and natural fibers—see Colchester (1991) and Braddock and O'Mahoney (1998).

20. A similar, dysfunctional bathroom scenario is also included in "La Comédie 2000," which Giacobbe produced for *Dazed and Confused* (December/January 2000). In this spread, a double-page opening represents a young girl with diabolic horns in the guise of Humanity and a man representing God both standing in baths of water while wearing their clothes.

21. Giacobbe's interest in science fiction is also exemplified in his cult pop video, "Revolution Action," for the Atari Teenage Riot. See http://www/scifi.com/exposure/frameup/revolutionaction.html.

22. Manfred E. Clynes and Nathan S. Kline coined the term "cyborg" (or cybernetic organism) to refer to "self-regulating man–machine systems" (Clynes and Kline 1960: 27). This enhanced cyborgian man could survive in extraterrestrial environments; and at the time of writing both authors were intensely concerned with the impact of space exploration on the human organism.

23. In Dick's narrative human beings are able to detect replicants because they possess the sense of empathy, which the replicants do not. In the film, it is not so much a lack of empathy that demarcates the replicant, but a lack of memories. For one of several illuminating studies of *Blade Runner*, see Kerman (1991).

24. Anne Balsamo, in Featherstone and Burrows (1995), mentions that a special issue of *Life* magazine in February 1989 called "Visions of Tomorrow" discussed the development of an artificial uterus. And at the time of writing this article, the House of Lords had just given its backing to the British government's legal order extending the types of disease that can be researched on human embryos under the 1990 Human Fertilization and Embryology Act (Hall and Radford 2001: 2).

25. Were it not for the picture's caption, it would be tempting to interpret this image as another that portrays Jason with Ketuta's head. (After all, the model is wearing a figure-masking, loose-fitting garment that could be worn by either a man or a woman.) In which case the double-take of *kairos* would mean that neither simply "man" nor "woman," but "man-woman," in the form of the hybrid character in Figure 1, will be the millennium's savior. It is this kind of deconstructed identity that Barthes (1995: 133) prefigured as the embodiment of a new social and sexual politics: ". . . once the alternative is rejected (once the paradigm is blurred) utopia begins: meaning and sex become the object of a free play, at the heart of which the (polysemant) forms and the (sensual) practices, liberated from the binary prison, will achieve a state of infinite expansion."

26. See, for example, Weber (1999), for a broader discussion of apocalyptic consciousness.

References

Barthes, R. 1995. *Roland Barthes*, London: Papermac.

Braddock, S. E. and M. O'Mahoney. 1998. *Techno Textiles*, London: Thames and Hudson.

Burgin, V. 1991. "Realising the Reverie." In *TEN.8*, Vol.2, No.2, pp. 8–15.

Clynes, M. E. and N. S. Kline. 1960. "Cyborgs and Space." *Astronautics*, September, pp. 26–7, 74–6.

Colchester, C. 1991. *The New Textiles*, London: Thames & Hudson.

Cole, B. 1997. "The Devil Inside." *i.D.*, November.

Cotton, C. 2000. *Imperfect Beauty: The Making of Contemporary Fashion Photographs*. London: V&A Publications.

Doane, M. A. 1990. "Technophilia: Technology, Representation and the Feminine." In M. Jacobus *et al.* (eds), *Body/Politics: Women and the Discourse of Science*. London: Routledge.

Eshun, E. 2000. "The Bold and the Beautiful." *The Guardian, Fashion Special*, Autumn–Winter.

Featherstone, M. and R. Burrows (eds). 1995. *Cyberspace, Cyberbodies, Cyberpunk—Cultures of Technological Embodiment*. London: Sage.

Flett, K. 2000. "altered images." *Life, The Observer Magazine*, 28 May.

Freud, S. 1985. "The Uncanny." In S. Freud, *Art and Literature*, pp. 335–76. Harmondsworth: Penguin.

Hall, S. and T. Radford. 2001. "Peers Vote To Permit New Research on Embryos." *The Guardian*, 23 January, p. 2.

Halliday, F. 2001. *The World at 2000*. Basingstoke: Palgrave.

Haraway, D. J. 1991. "A Cyborg Manifesto: Science, Technology, and Socialist-Feminism in the Late Twentieth Century." In *Simians, Cyborgs and Women*. London: Free Association Books.

——. 1997. *Modest Witness@Second Millenium. Femaleman© Meets Oncomouse™ Feminism and Technoscience*. London: Routledge.

Jay, M. and M. Neve. 1999. "Apocalypse then and now." *The Guardian (Saturday Review)*, 18 December, p. 3.

Jobling, P. 1999. *Fashion Spreads—Word and Image in Fashion Photography Since 1980*. London and New York: Berg.

Kelly, K. 1994. *Out of Control*, London: Fourth Estate Ltd.

Kerman, J. B. 1991. *Retrofitting Blade Runner*. Bowling Green: BGSU Popular Press.

Kermode, F. 1966. *The Sense of An Ending—Studies in the Theory of Fiction*. Oxford: Oxford University Press.

Kristeva, J. 1982. *Powers of Horror: An Essay in Abjection*. New York: Columbia University Press

La Gavin, F. 1999. "Lie Back and Think Of . . ." *Dazed and Confused*, November.

Lavin, M. 1993. *Cut with the Kitchen Knife—The Weimar Photomontages of Hannah Höch*. New Haven, CT and London: Yale University Press.

Mitchell, W. J. 1992. *The Reconfigured Eye: Visual Truth in the Post-Photographic Era*. Cambridge, MA: MIT Press.

Nordau, M. 1895. *Degeneration*. New York: D. Appleton and Co.

Penley, C. (1990). "Time, Travel, Primal Scene and the Critical Dystopia." In A. Kuhn (ed.), *Alien Zone: Cultural Theory and Contemporary Science Fiction Cinema*. London: Verso.

Perera, D. 2000. "Rostrum." *The Guardian* (*Education*), 17 October, p. 43.

Plato. 1974. *The Republic*. Harmondsworth: Penguin.

Porter, H. 1995. "Does Decency Have a Future? Or Have Values Had Their Day?" *The Independent on Sunday* (*Review*), 9 April, p. 20.

Riemschneider, B. (ed.). 1995. *Wolfgang Tillmans*. Cologne: Benedikt Taschen Verlag.

Roberts, S. 1999. "Breakthrough in Wearable Electronics." *Knitting International*, October, p. 17.

Scholes, R. 1980. ""Language, Narrative and Anti-Narrative." *Critical Inquiry*, Vol. 7, No. 1, Autumn.

Showalter, E. 1991. *Sexual Anarchy—Gender and Culture at the Fin de Siècle*. London: Bloomsbury.

Silver, L. 1998. *Remaking Eden: Cloning and Beyond in a Brave New World*. London: Weidenfeld.

Sontag, S. 1978. "The Avedon Eye," British *Vogue*, December, pp. 104–7.

Stokes, J. 1989. *In the Nineties*. Chicago: The University of Chicago Press.

TEN.8. 1991. "Digital Dialogues—Photography in the Age of Cyber-space." Vol. 2, No. 2.

Tillmans, W. 1998. *Burg*. Cologne: Taschen.

Weaver, M. 1984. *Julia Margaret Cameron 1815–1879*. London: The Herbert Press Ltd.

Weber, E. 1999. *Apocalypses: Prophecies, Cults and Millennial Beliefs Throughout the Ages*. London: Hutchinson.

Wilkie, T. 1991. "Mice embryos" sex changed." *The Independent*, 9 May, p. 1.

Wombell, P. (ed.). 1991. *PhotoVideo: Photography in the Age of the Computer*. London: Rivers Oram Press.

Fashion Theory, Volume 6, Issue 1, pp. 25–44
Reprints available directly from the Publishers.
Photocopying permitted by licence only.
© 2002 Berg. Printed in the United Kingdom.

"Put in Just for Pictures": Fashion Editorial and the Composite Image in *Nova* 1965–1975

Alice Beard

Alice Beard is Senior Lecturer
in Contextual Studies at the
Surrey Institute of Art and
Design and is currently
researching towards a Phd on
Nova Magazine 1965–1975 at
Goldsmiths College, University
of London.

With the re-launch of *Nova* in June 2000 into a saturated market and its seemingly inevitable demise, it seems timely to look back at the original to ascertain how its status today is reflected in its approach to magazine design. *Nova* enjoyed only a decade of publication in Britain, from 1965 to 1975, but in that time provided unprecedented space for creative talent, and enjoyed a relatively radical freedom of expression. *Nova's* first issue advertised itself as "A new kind of magazine for the new kind of woman" and made its appeal to "women who think magazines don't understand." In this article I will concentrate on two aspects of *Nova* that, at the time, distinguished its production from that of other magazines. These are the construction of fashion images and the content of fashion editorial.

While the recent *Nova* was suffused with the rhetoric of consumption, the former *Nova* could be seen to take a less rigid stance in relation to its advertisers and readership. *Nova* was a magazine to be owned, to be dismantled and reassembled and to be kept. *Nova*'s fashion editorial differed from other contemporary British magazines in a number of ways. In February 1970 readers were told "Fashion Needs Re-Thinking: Start Here (Figure 1)":

Figure 1
"Head for the Haberdashery!":
Re-thinking Fashion by
Caroline Baker, photograph by
Hans Feurer. The images were
positioned back to back
across three consecutive
double-page spreads. By
purchasing two copies of the
magazine and pasting the
images together a five-foot wall
poster could be made. This
page showed how the poster
would look when complete.
Nova, February 1970.

On the following pages we show, on three sections of the body, the accessories you can play around with. And if you want to see them worn almost life size, buy another *Nova* and join the pages together for a superb poster (February 1970).

The spread was photographed as three frames by Hans Feurer, the images positioned lengthways back to back across three consecutive double-page spreads; by buying two copies and pasting the images together a five-foot poster could be made. This use of a poster format, of the magazine itself as "assemblage," offers a different approach to the purpose and function of magazines. As one reader's comments suggested, rather than being a disposable item *Nova* was an object to be collected, she had kept a copy of May 1971, featuring a cut-along-the-dotted-lines, do-it-yourself flip-book photographed by Duffy entitled "How to undress for your husband":

> *Nova* is the only magazine that I have ever kept an issue of . . . I kept things as a record of social events and I think that what this is, it's a terrific record of the times. It was like a treat, an indulgence, I looked forward to it coming out, . . . I enjoyed having something that I felt was quite special . . . one might have left this out, for people to see on the table, you might have just displayed it, casually, but I wouldn't have left *Woman's Own* out, that was not quite what I wanted to be seen to be reading (Reader 1: M.W. 2000).

This study then, is about how and why these images have moved from the page to the kitchen wall, and how the treatment of fashion in *Nova* encouraged some form of further action beyond purchasing the clothing featured in the magazine. What will be proposed is that this very process was encouraged by an emphasis on visual form in the magazine, demonstrated by the inclusion of cut-out-and-keep flip-books, wall murals and posters, and, fundamentally, underpinned by the treatment of fashion by the magazine's production staff. For the art director, Harri Peccinotti,[1] fashion was dismissed as playing an incidental role: what was important were the visual possibilities the fashion spread offered:

> It was never a fashion magazine. It had twelve pages of fashion which was my idea to put in just for pictures. So when you flicked through the magazine, you would hit some pictures, somewhere— a block of colour. The fashion editor had free rein . . . The fashion photography in *Nova* was completely new compared to what was done in other magazines . . . At *Nova*, [the fashion pages] were almost an insult to fashion at times . . . the decision was made to put a twelve-page section of photographs in the magazine which could be outlandish. We chose fashion because it was an easy way to make a splash of colour (Williams 1998: 106).

Was fashion in *Nova* "put in just for pictures"? If so, how did the reader respond to this emphasis on the formal qualities of the fashion spread? In design writing (Owen 1991) and reader interviews[2] it is the "look" of the magazine that has been celebrated, as one reader remembered:

> Brilliant layout, visually it was superb, it was right away and fresh from all the other magazines available at the time . . . I have a visual image of it as an object, it stood out on the magazine stand . . . the printing was different, different typefaces, some sans serif stuff in there as you went through it, pictures right to the edge (Reader 2: J.T. 2000).

Sally Stein (1989) has proposed that context is the determinant of meaning in a magazine, and it should therefore be studied as a whole, rather than in its constituent parts. I have taken this approach as a methodological model for *Nova*'s analysis in an attempt to address the gaps left by previous readings of fashion photography, in particular its position within the magazine, and the specific consumption of these images by readers. This is problematic: there are inherent contradictions in reading images and applying meaning retrospectively; however, in an attempt to determine how the treatment of fashion in *Nova* was in some way "new," as it declared itself to be, my methodology has categorized the magazine's fashion features by type, encompassing editorial motivation, visual form, and reader usage. Through the process of this research a consistency has emerged in oral history and other primary source documentation, and it is hoped that, by naming the ambiguity, these contradictions can at least be teased out. What emerges is a sense of "authenticity" in a shared history revealed by both the readers and producers of *Nova*. This is how the magazine is remembered, even if it has not been formally articulated within the history of fashion.

My intention here is to shift analysis away from the decontextualized nature of readings that center the genius of individual photographers, as encapsulated by the sixties "photographer-hero" identified in Antonioni's *Blow-Up* (1966) and reinforced by many a glossy book and museum exhibition. Where magazines have been discussed outside the framework of the fashion photographer analysis has focused on distinct areas, the "formal textual features" (Ballaster 1991: 8) such as layout, tone of address and the distribution of advertising and editorial material, and the theme or subject of the magazine's content (Winship 1987). As a consequence, the aesthetic motivations of typography, layout, and composition have come to be marginalized.

The treatment of fashion in *Nova* can be categorized into three broad areas: the *Editorial Fashion Feature* (Figure 2), which took fashion as its subject but did not advertise or promote specific items; *Photo Story* fashion spreads (Figure 3), which were generally the commissioned shoots of renowned photographers whose work was not exclusive to *Nova*

Figure 2
"Goodbye to the Bra," Fashion Extra by Brigid Keenan, photographs by Philippe Tourjansky, *Nova,* November 1969.

and with which the academic writing on fashion photography has been primarily concerned; and finally the *Composite Image* fashion spread (Figure 4), which foregrounds its construction through montage and image manipulation. All these treatments, I will propose, emphasize a prioritization of form over content, and of image over product.

"The Way You Wear Your Clothes": Editorial Fashion Features

Characteristically, "editorial fashion features" in *Nova* profiled specific individuals and their relationship to clothing, and included articles on the subject of fashion without prices or stockist information. "Fashion was not in fashion"; rather, what seemed to be encouraged was choice and "fashionability" defined by "individuality" (Steele 1997: 280). Caroline Baker, who took over the position of fashion editor from Molly

Parkin in 1967, articulated this attitude in the cover article from February 1970; the by-line "Head for the Haberdashery" revealed the source of the accessories displayed:

> Fashions will go on changing endlessly . . . There is no one definitive "look" that can be said, with certainty, to be the 1970 look. Getting dressed has never been so much fun . . . you can make yourself into Jean Harlow, . . . and yet another day you can look as much like a man as you dare . . . Today it is the accessory that gives you away . . . that indicates fashionability, individuality. You need that very much as clothes become more mass produced. The way you wear your clothes, the belts and jewellery you add, has become the most important part of today's look (February 1970).

As Rosetta Brookes has observed: "Style ceases to be a matter of what you are wearing and becomes more the way you wear it" (Brookes 1989: 187). Fashion became "optional" in the Seventies (Steele 1997: 281). *Nova*'s July 1975 cover announced "Jeans: They're what life's all about," and Caroline Baker's article "You can take a blue jean anywhere" reveals the "anti-fashion" or "anti-product" approach adopted by *Nova*:

> . . . couturiers and fashion magazines report po-faced on this and that look, and we waver between what we think we should like and what we know we do like . . . The only thing that changes year to year is the gimmickry, and even that is of no great importance (July 1975).

This editorial text is significant as it reveals *Nova* defining itself in opposition to "fashion magazines." Cynthia White (1970) categorized *Nova* as a "features" magazine alongside *She*, rather than a "fashion" magazine like *Vogue*. We can gauge the effect of this type of fashion editorial in relation to coverage by other magazines from readers' memories: *Nova* "offered more than just fashion" (Reader 2: J.T. 2000). *Nova*'s influence it seems, was quite different; rather than the prescriptive advice offered by *19* or the "out of reach" clothing in *Vogue*, *Nova*'s fashion spreads provided inspiration and encouraged improvisation:

> They put together looks, it would be second hand stuff Portobello Road, street market . . . it was a good mix . . . a thinking woman's wardrobe if you like . . . there I was in the sticks in Plymouth, I'd come up to Bond Street and buy a pair of boots that would cost me all my wrapping cheese money on Saturday in the supermarket for a year, blow the lot on a pair of boots then put it together with second hand clothes and I felt like a million dollars . . . [*Nova* encouraged that:] you saw it in print and thought "Oh this is what I do, I like that, this is a good look, I'll buy a bit of fur and wrap

it around my ear," or whatever it was. Looking through the pages of *Vogue,* I was nowhere near that, I'm not that sort of person, but looking in here you thought, well, possibly . . . and you thought . . . "I could be part of this," much more than with *Vogue* (Reader 2: J.T. 2000).

This reader's self-identification with *Nova's* fashion content, defined through the process of "bricolage" (Hebdige 1979) as an activity, distances *Nova* from other contemporary magazines. In an interview for the publication accompanying the 1998 British Council fashion photography exhibition "Look at Me," Caroline Baker explained her role at *Nova,* reiterating the reader's own sentiments:

When I joined *Nova,* Dennis Hackett was the editor, and his brief to me was: "I just want you to go out there and do different things. I don't want it to look like *Vogue* or *Queen* or anything else. Your fashion pages are to be different." So I was encouraged to explore other avenues. I didn't have limitations. I was able to be more creative and crazy with the stories. At *Nova* I was pushed into alternative fashion because that was what the editor wanted. I never had any money, so I never shopped at Harrods. I was always looking for cheap clothes. I went to look at clothes in Portobello Road, and King's Road was a very happening place . . . There were a lot of secondhand clothes shops . . . I used to get girls to wear men's clothes. The army-surplus shop Lawrence Corner sold US uniforms. They were turning up by the bus load from Vietnam. That was the strength of *Nova,* we were exploring other avenues (Williams 1998: 103).

The fashion feature "Shop window dummies are good teachers" by Brigid Keenan from February 1970 reveals *Nova's* own editorial objectives. It suggested that shop window displays "do more these days than just sell clothes. They educate the public in a subtle way, they show what can be worn and how, they get people's eyes attuned to new looks, new ways of putting clothes together" (February 1970). This is the same endeavor as that of the fashion editorial in *Nova.* It was not just about advertising and selling clothes but more about encouraging fashionability and about "educating" its readers. The editorial letter from the first issue, March 1965, outlined the magazine's philosophy:

This is a magazine for women who make up their own minds. It is dedicated to the startling proposition that women have more to think about than what to do about dinner. Our theme is that a woman's life in 1965 is more interesting and more exciting than any escapism, so let's sit out the fantasy and make our entertainment out of reality (March 1965).

In attempting to address the "new woman," these explorations of "fantasy" and "reality" are continually negotiated in *Nova*'s fashion pages.

"This is a Good Look": The Photo Story

For the most part, critical writing concerned with fashion photography during this period emphasizes the photographer, much interesting analysis has been carried out on the work of, notably, Helmut Newton, Guy Bourdin, and Deborah Turbeville (Brookes 1997; Harrison 1991). In contemporary examinations and in retrospect, it was these photographers who seemed to epitomize the shift in fashion photography at this time. What is emphasized in critical analysis is the photographer, or the *auteur*, thereby removing the image from its original context between the pages of a magazine.

During the 1960s and 1970s a new style of fashion feature emerged, owing to the growing artistic autonomy of the photographer, who now had greater freedom and space to display individual style, supported by the backing of an editorial body. An increase in readership figures, more lucrative advertising budgets and the competition of television created the need to design more eye-catching images, as Nancy Hall-Duncan recognized: "since fashion photography is intended to create interest in its subject, new ways of creating memorable material had to be found" (Hall-Duncan 1979: 184). Increasing numbers of fashion photographers were moving into advertising, because they achieved relatively more creative freedom with larger working budgets; in response, editorial fashion needed to reinvent itself to compete.

In accordance with design change, the representations of fashion were transformed; a new angle and a new perspective was sought to attract attention and to signify design as desirable to the consumer. Advertising highlighted this shift, emphasizing the "product image" rather than the product itself. Rosetta Brookes has recognized a shift in fashion representation "from the product to the product-image" and offers as an explanation for the shift in fashion representation a reflection of consumer attitudes and the economic climate (Brookes 1989: 188). The criticism from designers was that their clothes were assuming a secondary position to the styling of the photograph. For the cause of reinvention, it was the image of fashion and of being fashionable that was being promoted, and not specifically clothes themselves. Ernestine Carter, *The Sunday Times Magazine* fashion editor, described the state of fashion photography by the end of the 1960s as imbued with a "mood of decadence" (Carter 1977: 146). Controversial fashion photography of the 1970s posed "the invitation to look" (Harrison 1991: 256), and as a result the clothes were often secondary to the prioritization of style and image.

The effect of contemporary cinematography was well reflected in the pages of *Nova,* as the editorial from the July 1973 feature "How the West was Worn" demonstrates. In image and text, readers were invited to "Study these photographs, the new wave of Westerns on TV and cinema screens and find the accessories to suit your own Western look. It's an easy look to acquire, as everyone must by now own at least one of the essentials" (July 1973). The themed shoot of this feature borrowed costume, location and postures from the Western genre. Over four double-page spread layouts, the models appear like characters, positioned centrally across the pages. The photograph bleeds to the edge of the page, in a format resonant of a big screen image. The models fill this space vertically. In its open-air setting there is a sense of a landscape inhabited by these women.

Writings concerning fashion photography during this period are concerned with the shift from traditional representation to themes of sexuality and violence, which invited from the reader a kind of "morbid curiosity." This language was already familiar from the cinema of the decade, and its influence was already apparent in the narrative qualities of much contemporary fashion photography. Sometimes this "violence" was not only explicit in the photographic image of fashion, but also implicit in its styling; by the use of harsh interior flash-lighting, the violation of extreme close-ups or the mutilation of the image by cropping. For many viewers, violence and sexuality in the visual media were empirically linked with glamor, and therefore presented an effective selling-point. *The Eyes of Laura Mars* (Irvin Kershner 1978) borrowed both subject-matter and visual aesthetic from these contemporary concerns. American cinema was undoubtedly influential, and films within the horror genre, with their representations of urban violence, resonated with a stylized glamor.

Martin Harrison (1991) has quoted Stephen Farber's *New York Magazine* article of 1976 in reference to the development of sexual and violent themes in fashion photography; but this explanation can also be ascribed to any photograph that offers some alternative to realism, or that tempts the viewer into a fantasy world:

> One of the functions of popular art has always been to give people some notion of experiences denied them in reality—a taste of danger. But perhaps as everyday life becomes more smoothly homogenised, people need splashier, more grotesque vicarious thrills (Farber 1976: 181).

Often in *Nova*'s "photo story" spreads this "experience denied in reality" is manifested not in themes of sex and violence, but rather in images of fantasy, conjured up by both word and picture, as the text accompanying Deborah Turbeville's "A Touch of Ballet Class" from *Nova*'s December 1973 issue demonstrates:

A party dress and perfect poise. Glamorous, flamboyant, extravagant—this season you can really dress it up. Never have evening gowns been so gorgeous, so original, so beautiful. Wear them extravagantly—the extrovert personal touch is 1974—and dramatically with a ballerina's stance and dancing accessories. Make floating entrances, sensational exists—would you turn down the chance to be a prima donna for a night? (December 1973)

In *Nova*'s "photo story" features, fashion is subservient to aesthetic and visual form; clothing is not displayed clearly, but rather acts as costume for the narrative of the image. The tendency toward retrospective style and styling further mystifies the more exclusive clothing ranges that feature in these types of spread. Sarah Moon's photographs for "Old Graces Never Die" from October 1972 (Figure 3) resemble stills cut from

Figure 3
"Old Graces Never Die": The antique look for young ladies. Fashion by Caroline Baker, photograph by Sarah Moon, *Nova*, October 1972.

a filmic sequence: they evoke a sense of narrative or story. This element of fantasy is emphasized by hazy effects, soft focus, a grainy image, subdued lighting overly washed out, and dramatically contrasting shadows. Retrospective styling here equates with dream-like sequences to present an expensive clothing range featuring designer, hand-made and antique clothing. The exclusive "specialness" of these items is also often reinforced in the accompanying editorial. The text by Caroline Baker for Terence Donovan's photographs for "The Limpid Line," June 1973 reads:

> Edging into fashion: the "H" line. Waists are dropping to hip level, hems to mid-calf. Willowy, limpid, tube-like, this is a natural move away from the stiffer fashions. Pablo & Delia, the two talented designers who are responsible for this new look, work independently producing small collections which are totally different from current fashions but which will have a strong influence on next season's clothes. Before the look becomes commonplace buy the original, or anything droopy from the very few designers at present on the same wavelength. Or you can improvise with "antique" clothes—for this new look, like so many, has a touch of the retrospective about it (June 1973).

The traditional use of illustration in girls' and women's magazines (Walkerdine 1984), usually to accompany fiction or short stories opens up the possibilities of imagination and fantasy. Narrative "photo story" photography in *Nova* operated in much the same way, using clothing as a prop and inviting the reader to suspend belief. By setting the scene outside the present and locating it in the "other" it was removed from real time and real life.

"Let's Sit Out the Fantasy": The Composite Fashion Image

> One woman in her day plays many parts . . . So here follows, in eight acts, presented with enormous admiration, one woman's fairly average day, and a small selection of the parts she plays in it. Full costume details given throughout (March 1965).

The editorial accompanying the fashion feature "One woman in her day" from *Nova*'s first issue acknowledges the masquerade of femininity, the text itself referring to "play," "costume" and the different "roles" available to the modern woman. Read in the same context as the opening editorial statement, which voiced the magazine's desire to "sit out the fantasy," it also highlights the contradictions raised by attempting to address and define the "new woman." In contrast to the "photo story," the "composite fashion image" in *Nova* (Figure 4) exists very much in

Figure 4
"12 Pages to Make you Think About Colour": Fashion by Molly Parkin, photographs by Harri Peccinotti, *Nova,* August 1966.

the present, and often provides visual humor and fun. As Parkin has explained "I had been allowed, indeed encouraged, at *Nova* to approach fashion with some degree of humor. I didn't feel *Vogue* had its tongue sufficiently in its cheek" (Parkin 1993: 182). It is the composite image that seems to most conform with the magazine's objectives to make "entertainment out of reality." Photomontage and the manipulated image within *Nova*'s fashion editorial point to an accentuated realism by acknowledging their own material medium, in contrast to the photo story, which avoids drawing attention to the surface of the picture plane or material construction, its focus resolutely on the subject. The themed seamless images of the "photo story" function as a window opening into a fantasy world. Whereas the "composite image" creates a screen or layer that separates the viewer from the product, disrupting the viewing process by calling attention to its construction and thereby, to its existence as a "construct."

While we can describe the fashion pages of *Nova* as the photographic depiction of clothing, this analysis of the "composite image" positions the photograph as only one element of the overall design of the spread. Within *Nova*'s pages both the fashion photograph and the fashion product are subordinated to an element of graphic design. Rather than this design's existing merely as a tool for information disclosure, it emerges as an autonomous aesthetic, foregrounded in its layout and importance, and becomes in effect both content and subject. Molly Parkin, *Nova*'s first fashion editor, has articulated this approach clearly by suggesting: "I had never, in truth, been very interested [in fashion] . . . I only ever saw clothes in terms of shape and colour" (Parkin 1993: 193). In fact it seems that even the color of models was considered as contributing to the graphic design of the page. As David Hillman has subsequently revealed, this is demonstrated in "12 pages to make you think about colour" (Figure 4); he states; "It was meant to be twelve pages of black girls in colour clothes" (Gibbs 1993: 54). The contemporary editorial text itself also made this point: "strong colours need living up to; they can easily dominate the woman inside unless she herself is as vivid in personality or colouring. For this reason we photographed the following sportswear on dark-skinned girls" (August 1966). These formal preoccupations appeared to have been overreached by Molly Parkin, with the proposal for a fashion story she credits for her final dismissal:

> White on white—white-skinned models with bleached blonde hair flown in from Scandinavia, preferably albinos, wearing all-white clothes. White linen suits, white cotton frocks, white satin chemises, white chiffon dance-dresses, white maribou mufflers. We'll fly them to the Alps and photograph them against the snow, just before dawn when the light is pure white (Parkin 1993: 181).

For Molly Parkin color as a graphic element would often take priority over content, and we can see evidence of this in *Nova* from 1965 to 1967 in the division of fashion pages into what she termed "colour zones" (Parkin 1993: 181). The use of color as form that subsumes content reached its peak in May 1974 with the publication of a *Blue Nova*, containing twelve blue-themed editorial features, twenty-four pages actually printed in blue ink (editorial text, images and advertising), and a ten-page fashion spread entitled "Blue Chip Investments." The cover simply declared: "It's time you were thinking blue thoughts," and as the editorial address revealed: "Once in a *Blue Nova* . . . Yes, once and once only, we present, for your entertainment and delight, a blue magazine" (May 1974). There seemed little justification as to the choice of color theme other than the brief explanation that "Blue is our favourite colour."

Bordwell and Thompson's examination of space and form in film[3] identifies certain editing practices that can be set against the paradigm of "ordinary usage" this provides a useful comparison to the approach *Nova* takes in its representation of fashion. As they observed in the work of Japanese director Ozu, the:

> most radical uses of space lack both "compositional" motivation (i.e. motivation according to narrative economy) and "realistic" motivation (i.e. motivation according to canons of verisimilitude); the motivation is purely "artistic." Space, constructed alongside and sometimes against the cause/effect sequence, becomes "foregrounded" to a degree that renders it at times the primary structural level of the film (Bordwell and Thompson 1976: 45).

Techniques in *Nova*'s composite fashion images such as the use of intermediate space and a focus on imagery with no "product" value; the deployment of color as an object without conventional symbolism; and the inclusion of empty or insignificant space result in an "uneconomical" use of the page that is not motivated by content (in this case the product). It is the formal aspects of the design that are foregrounded and that exist as autonomous structures within the spread. The use of clothing and accessories in *Nova*'s composite fashion spreads is also comparable to the *mise-en-scène* in the "collage novels" of Robbe-Grillet as analyzed by Roland Barthes, who suggests: "if the object is here the function of something, it is not the function of its natural destination . . . but of a visual itinerary" (Barthes 1972: 15–16). The attention to the formal qualities of design in *Nova* received criticism, with one journalist complaining in 1969 that the magazine had "pictures and type-patterns subduing the words on every page" (Hutt 1970: 224).

Nova has been compared to *The Sunday Times Magazine* for its innovative design (Owen 1991), and this comparison is perhaps due in part to the employment of the art director David Hillman, who moved from the magazine to *Nova* in June 1969, bringing with him stylistic devices that would be further explored: primarily the use of photomontage. *Nova*'s use of the "manipulated" image can be aligned with Andy Grundberg's definition of the Parisian surrealists who, through collage and montage "intervene in the photographic process [both] during development and after" (Grundberg 1990: 81), and whose work displayed an emphasis on the constructed image, in contrast to "the modernist aesthetic of so-called straight photography, which prohibited any manipulation of the transaction between the subject and the film" (Grundberg 1990: 82). The latter approach to photography can be applied to the *Sunday Times Magazine*'s use of the photograph more for its possibilities of documentary record than for any graphic aesthetic. Unlike seamless photomontages, which make strange their subject through unlikely associations and contexts, the photomontages in *Nova* generally foregrounded and made a subject of their construction. For Grundberg, the composite image: "supplies a rationale both for photography's position within the art world and for those photographic practices that seek to disorient and disrupt our conventional responses to images" (Grundberg 1990: 86). The political practice of montage has been both well utilized and well documented. In contrast to those images that construct fantasy and masquerade the reality of their nature, the foregrounded construction of montage in effect reveals the "real":

> Advertising produces an image whereby you fall into a seamless world. A world where there is no risk to your identity, no problems, no struggle, no conflict. An advertisement may play with meaning, it may produce the fantastic, but all in all it rarely challenges how we see ourselves as individuals. Advertisements place the viewer (consumer) as though s/he were the centre of the world; it ultimately reassures one of one's precious individuality. The issue is about those montages which attempt to foreground their construction and which do not close everything off, making it all fit into a neat unified whole (Lomax and Myers 1983: 4).

"We Used to Wallpaper our Kitchen with It": Use of the Fashion Spread

> "Buy two *Novas*, join the fashion pages together and you have a beautiful seven-foot frieze" (April 1972).

The inclusion of pull-out wall murals (Figure 1), where readers were invited to buy multiple copies of an issue to make up friezes and posters, as well as to cut out and make up flip-books, encouraged some form of further action beyond purchasing the clothing featured:

> It encouraged you to be more experimental, or even, to carry it a step further, people might look at some of the photographs as art forms . . . they were beautiful . . . I'd cut out photos from the magazines simply because the photographs were stunning or because the photographer had captured a certain mood, or because of the colours, it doesn't necessarily have to be what he's photographing that makes the picture, and that came over in the magazine (Reader 2: M.W. 2000).

"12 p-p-p-pages to make you think about c-c-c-colour," photographed and art directed by Harri Peccinotti (Figure 4) is a "composite image" constructed of three photographs that have been cropped and repeated on the page. In the top left image the repetition accentuates the broad horizontal stripes of the racing vests; in the bottom left it is the shape and length of the girls' legs and boxing boots that is seemingly extended in triplication; while in the bottom right corner repetition draws attention to the contrasted lettering on the cycling shorts. These clothes, it would appear, have been chosen for their graphic qualities; their design is foregrounded by the repetition of specific motifs and patterns. As the accompanying text reveals "The design and cost of these clothes are extremely good, but they are featured mainly as an exercise in exciting colour combinations" (August 1966).

In the photograph of a reader's living-room from 1968 (Figure 5), we can see evidence that this montage has been taken further. The photographic images from "12 pages" have been cut out and reused to form a new "spread" that is displayed on a cork board above the dining table. If we look closely we can see that the image from the bottom left of the *Nova* feature has been removed and cut out along the first repetition. Where this division was a white line in the original in the reader's assemblage space is left on the cork board to reinforce the "seam" visually. If we look to the top left of the assemblage we can see that the original photograph has been cropped vertically, so that it reveals just two of the models and none of the product information. What is kept, however, is the blank space of the page's edge to the left, resulting in a visual emphasis on the pattern constructed by shape, line and color. This usage and re-usage of the magazine is supported by other readers' recollections:

Figure 5
Pin-board display including images taken from "12 Pages to Make you Think About Colour," reader photograph from 1968.

> We used to wallpaper the walls with it, our kitchen was completely covered with pictures, really beautiful images from *Nova*, text and pictures, the layout, typography, it was lovely to look at then. We use them as art, I actually framed them visually . . . some of the standard of layout was incredibly artistic and in a frame or used in a collage it became art (Reader 2: J.T. 2000).

Collage can be positioned as a cultural form that appropriates imagery from mass culture, re-presents it, and then feeds it back into the mainstream as both process and aesthetic. In his analysis of art and culture in 1960s Britain, Robert Hewison has stressed the importance of the technique of collage as a medium constructed of "material that has come from anywhere, and may return to anywhere . . . The work is an object . . . it asks to be taken as an object in itself without deeper allusions. You are expected to take an object as it is, and enjoy it for itself, without associations" (Hewison 1986: 51–2). However, it was the inherent associations of *Nova* and its content that seemed to motivate its reuse. As Roger Cardinal proposes, the practice of collage can be viewed as a form of collecting: "Both (collage and collecting) ultimately exist to be shown, and implicitly to be shown to impress. We can say that both aspire to be noticed, inspected, admired, even envied" (Cardinal 1994: 71). *Nova,* as a magazine in this reader's usage, assigns itself to Cardinal's point:

> We all did these notice boards, you would pin up nice post cards, interesting pictures, cut out bits from magazines, add things, change them around. With *Nova* I remember it was a magazine that was good, it was visually stylish, smart. it was about style and image, I suppose by buying it and having it you thought you were more exclusive, part of the fabric of the whole thing (Reader 3: J.B. 2000).

Reader interviews have described *Nova* in enthusiastic and celebratory terms: as a defining moment in their lives. While oral history is problematic, these recollections have been carried with the magazine's readers. If *Nova* appears both romanticized and/or mythologized, this nevertheless acknowledges its powerful symbolism, as readers find themselves today, in part, still identified through, and with, their relationship to the magazine. *Nova* can then be placed within a framework that acknowledges that material culture (Appadurai 1986; Prown 1988) not only signifies but constructs and essentially maintains lived experience.

It has been argued that *Nova*'s fashion features did not endorse specific items of clothing, but promoted style, and encouraged "fashionability," rather than dictating what exactly to wear. Clothes were subservient to the image, the aesthetic of the spread prioritized over representation of the featured garments. Often, as in the "composite image," valuable page space was filled with repetitions and distortions of a single outfit, manipulated and cropped: attention called to the surface of the image. Other fashion spreads were both self-conscious and self-reflexive, with an emphasis on the models' "acting out" of roles for the camera/viewer. Retrospective, thematic and filmic styling in these "photo stories" emphasized a "look" through the construction of narrative, with the clothes as props forming part of the filmic *mise-en-scène*. These alongside the "fashion editorial"—cropped, blown up, enlarged, made "unreal"— all point toward a knowing illusion where the construction of what is represented is itself acknowledged, and where the medium dominates the message. As a result, Peccinotti's claim that fashion in *Nova* was "Put in just for pictures . . . an easy way to make a splash of colour" can be clearly demonstrated in this prioritization of image over product and form over content.

Notes

1. Harri Peccinotti was Art Director from 1965 to 1967 and was retained as a photographer when David Hillman took over the position.
2. Three readers are quoted in this text: Readers 1 and 2 are women who were both in their early twenties at *Nova*'s launch in 1965. *Reader* 1, M.W., was from a middle-class background; she lived in Birmingham with her husband and worked as a reservations attendant for BOAC. *Reader* 2, J.T., was from a working-class background and lived in Plymouth until she moved to London to go to art school; she lived with a student friend. While these women alone are in no way indicative of actual readership, they do represent the intended audience as outlined in the dummy issue and statements of editorial intent published in contemporary trade press such as the *World's Press News*. The photograph (Figure 5) was taken in 1968 by Reader 3, J.B., who was from a working-class community in Wales. After studying in London he moved to Buckinghamshire, where he lived with his wife and taught art at a school. He recalls the taking of the photograph: "I wasn't aiming at any particular composition, it was just a snap shot taken on the Sunday morning after a party the night before."
3. Bordwell and Thompson offer an analysis of the of the Japanese director Ozu Yasujiro's films set against a paradigm of classical Hollywood cinema, dictated by the "continuity style," which is taken here to be the familiar "ordinary usage" of cinema and the dominant framework by which most films were made. This analysis distinguishes Ozu's films by their difference and "deviation" from "classical" filmic conventions, and it is through this contrast that specific formal practices are revealed. Bordwell and Thompson propose that, set against this paradigm "the modernity of Ozu's work involves the use of specific spatial devices which challenge the supremacy of narrative causality" (Bordwell and Thompson 1976: 44).

Acknowledgments

I would like to thank Sally Alexander and Carol Tulloch for their support and advice during the research and writing of this article.

References

Appadurai, A. 1986. *The Social Life of Things*. Cambridge: Cambridge University Press.

Ballaster, Ros et al. 1991. *Women's Worlds: Ideology, Femininity and the Women's Magazine*. London: Macmillan.

Barthes, Roland. 1972. *Critical Essays*. Evanston, IL: Illinois University Press.

Bordwell, David and Kirsten Thompson. 1976. "Space and Narrative in the Films of Ozu." *Screen*, vol. 17, no. 2.

Brookes, Rosetta. 1989. "Sighs and Whispers in Bloomingdales: A Review of a Mail-Order Catalogue for their Lingerie Department," in *Zoot Suits and Second-Hand Dresses: An Anthology of Fashion and Music*, ed. Angela McRobbie. London: Macmillan.

——. 1997. "Fashion: Double-Page Spread," in *The Camerawork Essays*, ed. Jessica Evans. London: Rivers Oram.

Cardinal, Roger. 1994. "Collecting and Collage-making: The Case of Kurt Schwitters," in *The Cultures of Collecting*, ed. John Elsner and Roger Cardinal. London: Reaktion.

Carter, Ernestine. 1977. *The Changing World of Fashion*. London: Weidenfeld and Nicolson.

Farber, Stephen. 1976. "The Bloody Movies; Why Film Violence Sells." *New York Magazine*, 29 September.

Gibbs, David (ed.). 1993. *Nova 1965–1975*. London: Pavilion.

Grundberg, Andy. 1990. "On the Dissecting Table: The Unnatural Coupling of Photography and Surrealism," in *The Critical Image: Essays on Contemporary Photography*, ed. Carol Squiers. Seattle, WA: Bay Press.

Hall-Duncan, Nancy. 1979. *The History of Fashion Photography*. New York: Alpine Books.

Harrison, Martin. 1991. *Appearances: Fashion Photography Since 1945*. London: Jonathan Cape.

Hebdige, Dick. 1979. *Subculture: The Meaning of Style*. London: Methuen.

Hewison, Robert. 1986. *Too Much: Art and Society in the Sixties 1960–1975*. London: Methuen.

Hutt, Allen. 1970. "The First Word on Magazine Design." *Penrose Annual*, vol. 63. London: Lund Humphries.

Lomax, Yves and Kathy Myers. 1983. "Photography and Graphic Design." *Camerawork*, 24.

Owen, William. 1991. *Magazine Design*. London: Lawrence King.

Parkin, Molly. 1993. *Moll: The Making of Molly Parkin*. London: Victor Gollancz.

Prown, J. D. 1988. "Mind in Matter: An Introduction to Material Culture Theory and Method," in *Material Life in America 1600–1860*, ed. R. Blair St George. Boston: North Eastern University Press.

Steele, Valerie. 1997. "Anti-Fashion: The 1970s." *Fashion Theory: The Journal of Dress, Body & Culture*. September, Vol. 1, Issue 3.

Stein, Sally. 1989. "The Graphic Ordering of Desire: Modernisation of a Middle Class Magazine," in *The Contest of Meaning: Critical Histories of Photography*, ed. Richard Bolton. Cambridge, MA: MIT Press.

Walkerdine, Valerie. 1984. "Some Day my Prince Will Come: Young Girls and the Preparation for Adolescent Sexuality," in *Gender and Generation*, ed. Angela McRobbie and Mica Nava. London: Macmillan.

White, Cynthia. 1970. *Women's Magazines 1693–1968*. London: Michael Joseph.

Williams, Val (ed.). 1998. *Look at Me: Fashion Photography in Britain 1960 to the Present*. London: British Council.

Winship, Janice. 1987. *Inside Women's Magazines*. London: Pandora Press.

Fashion Theory, Volume 6, Issue 1, pp. 45–60
Reprints available directly from the Publishers.
Photocopying permitted by licence only.
© 2002 Berg. Printed in the United Kingdom.

Looking American: Louise Dahl-Wolfe's Fashion Photographs of the 1930s and 1940s

Rebecca Arnold

Rebecca Arnold is a Senior
Lecturer in Fashion History and
Theory at Central Saint Martins
College of Art and Design in
London.

Louise Dahl-Wolfe outlined her attitude to photography in her memoirs of 1984, in which she wrote:

> The camera is a medium of light, one that actually paints with light. In using the spotlights with reflecting lights, I could control the quality of the forms revealed to build a composition. Photography to my mind is not a fine art. It is splendid for recording a period in time, but it has definite limitations, and the photographer certainly doesn't have the freedoms of a painter (Dahl-Wolfe 1984: 86–7).

Dahl-Wolfe's down-to-earth approach and love of clear, flattering lighting schemes, which showed both model and outfit to their best advantage, made her popular with women's magazine readers and advertisers. Her career stretched from 1933 to 1960 and thus encompassed a turbulent period in American history, from the Depression to the Second World War to the start of the Cold War. Yet as a photographer who focused principally on fashion, working mainly for *Harper's Bazaar* and *Vogue*, her photographs rarely refer explicitly to current events. Instead, they represent and help to shape feminine identities that evoke myths of America: the pull between visions of a vast Edenic landscape of opportunity and the cosmopolitan modernity of the city. Dahl-Wolfe joined *Harper's Bazaar* in 1936, four years after Carmel Snow took over the publication and, with the art director Alexey Brodovitch, revolutionized its outlook, creating a visually ground-breaking magazine of fashion and culture, which brought its readers a modern, American view of life shaped by the European avant-garde. Dahl-Wolfe's images represent this dynamic of America equaling modernity, but her photographs were never so experimental as to intimidate the viewer. She was influenced by contemporary documentary style, the desire for pure, straight, honest images of "presentness." However, her work always remained the photography of fashion, with clothing central to its construction: designs are never blurred or abstracted in order to represent dynamism or movement.

Her photographs provide a rich source for examining the growing confidence of the New York fashion trade and the crystallization of the "American Look," which framed national identity in terms of active sportswear that spoke of functionalism and freedom. Dahl-Wolfe's warm color schemes and light-filled images present a fiction of stability and cohesion during a period of turmoil. They smooth away contradiction and anxiety, providing unproblematic and coherently constructed ideals of American femininity.

Images provide narratives of a culture, clues and revelations of the way a social group or indeed a nation envisions itself, particular to time and space. Dana Polan begins his book, *Power and Paranoia, History, Narrative and the American Cinema 1940–1950*, with a comparison of two facing pages of *Life* magazine from 13 August 1945. One page shows a series of black-and-white photographs of a Japanese soldier being killed with a flame-thrower by an Australian soldier, the other a color advertisement for Campbell's mushroom soup. The interlocking yet shockingly different narratives of these pictures demonstrate the extremes that cohabit in a culture that was increasingly dominated by visual images, where life itself was defined by representations of in turn banal and traumatic emblems of American identity. In discussing these images of the post-war experience, Polan contrasted the destructive certainties of war with the promise of consumerism, and stated: "Between the two images, within their differences, we can read an attempt to represent a certain social positioning, the fixities of a system, the delegation of roles, the assignation of goals" (Polan 1986: 6–7).

In this article, part of a longer, ongoing work in progress,[1] I want to analyze Louise Dahl-Wolfe's fashion photographs, which express the kind of propositions that Polan discussed. I want to consider how they position women, as model and as spectator, and how they may be interpreted in terms of America's goals. As fashion images they provide a rich source for both looking at women and looking at America. I intend to use fashion photographs as texts to be compared to other visual and documentary evidence of the period. So, rather than providing an exhaustive account of Dahl-Wolfe's work and life,[2] I aim to look at specific images from the 1930s and 1940s and consider how they might be contextualized geographically, historically and socially. Through a study of these photographs, I will seek greater understanding of the ways America saw itself during this period and the complex process of "making" American identity.

America/American

Leaning her arm against the back of the chair, the model pauses while writing a postcard (Figure 1). The card, a scene of a Spanish-style town

Figure 1
Harper's Bazaar, December 1938. Mary Sykes in Puerto Rico, 1938. Photograph by Louise Dahl-Wolfe. © 1989 Center for Creative Photography, Arizona Board of Regents. Collection Center for Creative Photography, The University of Arizona.

square, distinguishes her status as a tourist, while her stance speaks of her cultural authority. She is coolly nonchalant, one leg crossed over the other, pressed against the neatly decorated cloth of the outdoor café table at which she sits. Other cards lie strewn on the table, a flower has been tucked in the breast pocket of her casual, crisp cotton top, her matching skirt is practical, knee-length, with useful side pockets ready to collect further mementoes as she explores the area. The flat, bright light and dark shadows cast by her chair hint at midday heat. Her hair is swept from her face and wrapped in a scarf; white-rimmed sunglasses provide a contrast to her tanned skin and detach her from her surroundings. The squares woven into the tablecloth are echoed in the oversized checkerboard tiles of the floor that extends behind her, and together they provide a graphic pull to the center of the photograph, to her lithe figure. Her relaxed demeanor and simple, sporty clothing place her as an American. This Louise Dahl-Wolfe image was photographed in Puerto Rico in 1938, and demonstrates the ease with which the white North American, clad in streamlined functional clothing, may take possession of any environment, making it knowable to the spectator. The "otherness" of a variety of settings, South America in the 1930s, North Africa in the 1950s, is smoothed away, reduced to graphic designs that provide contrast for simple dresses, or perfect white-washed walls glowing in sunshine that sparkle behind a monochrome playsuit. For Dahl-Wolfe exotic locations were a means to enliven what she called the "pearl of little price" (Dahl-Wolfe 1984: 37), an outfit by a third-rate designer that needed to be made more visually enticing. In this instance, as was often the case at this period, the designer is not named; only the fabric is captioned, as "Wamsutta's Kanaka cloth." Potential anxieties about other cultures and other identities are allayed; the world becomes comprehensible, inhabitable, as long as the veneer of Americanness is maintained in the clear lines of the clothes. The composition and lighting are kept equally clean, apparently revealing all in the camera's gaze, yet actually acting as a mask to conceal the "other," allowing the relaxed American to prevail.

For a national identity to be constructed in such a huge and diverse country as America, the spectator must have an investment of belief in the mythic imagery that surrounds her. At this period American identity was defined in a series of often contradictory ideas of modernity, dynamism, progress and the city, alongside nostalgic evocations of the mythic West and dreams of opportunity. Imagery of the city and of the vastness of the American countryside were combined with representations of tanned, healthy bodies that linked the human figure to nature. Neil Campbell and Alasdair Kean wrote in 1997 of the impossibility of a single, stable American identity, yet pointed out that: "The rapid growth of industrialization and urbanization—the outward signs of modernity—encouraged the articulation of the nation as whole and unified in order that production and economic growth could develop around goals, shared beliefs and a sense of cohesion" (Campbell and Kean 1997: 21).

The need to create and maintain a stable identity stretched from the nineteenth into the twentieth century, as wars and economic depression meant that the government and industry needed to create a sense of common goals, while the public looked to myths of America to assuage anxieties. The growth of the media in the 1930s meant that a larger percentage of America's population was united by access to radio soaps, comic books, cinema and confession magazines. As Sheila Rowbotham noted, "An American popular identity took shape during the 1930s through the mass media, which increasingly aimed at women" (Rowbotham 1999: 214).

The dreams and desires of consumer culture numbed the pains of the period's hardships. The proliferation of photographs in magazines like *Life*, which was first published in 1936, acted as ciphers of the times as well as visual enticements to fantasize and consume. Andy Grundberg in his biography of Alexey Brodovitch cites *Life* magazine as the initiator of an era "in which photographs would be a major source of news, information and cultural iconography" (Grundberg 1989: 115). Like other authors, he links this to the historical context of the thirties, and continues by saying that "This intense interest in photographs and their appearance on the printed page was part of a wider revolution in visual consciousness. The increasing ease, economy, and sophistication of printing, and the development of better halftone reproduction technology, fuelled the demand for images of all sorts" (Grundberg 1989: 117).

People were encouraged to formulate both their own identities and that of America around repeated motifs of modernity, unity and progress. Americans could now view images of themselves simultaneously in popular magazines and on television in depictions that expressed their fears as well as their desires. The images shown reinforced Americanness as uniformly white, presenting an identity that ignored the nation's ethnic diversity.

The grim realities of the Depression were documented in the Farmer's Security Association's (FSA) exhaustive photographic survey of poverty and starvation, while the popular media explored escape routes that brought together myths of America. As Levine said, "This ambivalent yearning to combine the innocence and clarity of the past with the sophistication and technological complexity of the present can be discerned throughout modern American culture but was particularly strong in the 1930s" (Levine 1988: 28).

Within fashion this pull was articulated through contrasting imagery of nature and the city in editorial shoots, which will be addressed later in this article, but also in the industry's attempts to assert an American identity in dress that was distinct from the Old World luxury of couture. Dorothy Shaver, vice-president of the Lord and Taylor department store in New York, initiated a series of influential window displays promoting American designers; the first, in 1932, presented the work of Elizabeth

Hawes, along with a photograph of the designer. This signaled the slow move towards recognition for designers of New York ready-to-wear as individuals rather than, as was usual, as an anonymous figure behind a manufacturer's or department store's range. The shift towards clothing being sold mainly on the basis of a well-known designer's signature and personality was not to achieve predominance in America for several decades to come; editorial and advertising promotions in magazines only gradually followed Shaver's lead in naming specific designers.

However, it is significant that in the 1930s the fashion industry instituted more visible methods of selling American design on its own merits, rather than on its relationship to Parisian couture originals. This fulfilled a psychological need for more confident assertions of American identity in fashion design and a coherent sense of self that would come to fruition during the Second World War, when Paris was cut off from the rest of the world. It was also a response to various economic and industrial developments. During the Depression simple, plain fabrics, previously outside the realms of high fashion, began to gain favor. They were used in Paris by Chanel and Patou, but also increased their fashion status in New York, the fashion center of America since the 1820s, and by this point the focus for the crystallization of the "American Look."

While various styles of fashion were popular during this period, catering for the wide variety of women in America, it was sportswear-based, functional clothing that was to come to represent the way America saw itself. This was partly because it expressed ideals of youth, vitality and freedom, which linked to the American Dream, but also for sound economic reasons: simple clothes in sturdy fabrics are easier and cheaper to mass-produce. Caroline Rennolds Milbank notes in her exhaustive account, *New York Fashion, The Evolution of the American Look*, that in the 1930s "What caused a major change in the way American women were clothed is that manufacturers and retailers came to rely less on buying Paris originals that were expensive to import and to have copied by seamstresses earning American wages and more on what they could produce at home, independent of the French influence" (Milbank 1996: 98).

Mass production on a vast scale also provided mass access to fashionable clothing, and this democracy of availability became a selling point in itself, since it was promoted as an example of America's equal opportunities. Never mind that clothes were not always well made or well designed (as Dahl-Wolfe's "pearls of little price" testifies), belief in egalitarian ideals meant that New York ready-to-wear was read as a signifier of democracy.

The sleek American style, shown on athletic young models, also worked well with the new photographic styles of the period. In 1923 Edward Steichen had been appointed Photography Editor-in-Chief at Condé Nast, overseeing *Vogue* and *Vanity Fair*, and his glimmering images of flappers brought a feeling of new feminine independence and modernity to the pages of fashion magazines. Baron de Meyer's soft-focus Edwardian fantasies seemed increasingly out of sync with the crisp lines of modernist style, and once Snow and Brodovitch began to revamp *Harper's Bazaar*, fashion photography moved into a new era, led by New York-based photographers like Martin Munkacsi, who brought dynamic movement to the printed page. Nancy Hall-Duncan sees the latter's work as crucial in the development of a type of "honest" fashion photography that suited the energetic style of American fashion better than the rarefied sophistication of Parisian couture.

Louise Dahl-Wolfe's work encapsulates this relaxed mood, as well as highlighting the distinction between the way French couture and American ready-to-wear can be depicted. Her own photographs of couture provide luxurious images of elegant models, frequently set against paintings and backdrops that link them to the European history of art. One from 1949 seems to reinforce the historicized interior as the natural habitat for couture. A model clad in a ruby red, silk velvet suit by Dior glances haughtily down, hands on hips, ready to receive the viewer's gaze, yet contemptuous of the admiration her elegantly thin figure might provoke (Figure 2). The suit's skirt is, to quote the caption "bone narrow," drawing

Figure 2
Harper's Bazaar, September 1949. Suit: Christian Dior; Jewels: Cartier. Photograph by Louise Dahl-Wolfe. Courtesy of The Museum of the Fashion Institute of Technology, New York.

attention to the model's long legs and red satin ankle-strap sandals. The jacket fits her torso, flaring into a peplum at the waist, the jeweled Cartier parakeet brooch emphasizing her tiny waist. She is the epitome of ladylike style, with crimson gauntlet gloves and hair neatly coiled into her neck. Her face is a mask of perfection; delicate white skin, pout-red lips and a sweep of black eyeliner. She is illuminated by a glow of bright light, which casts half her face into darkness and extends a long shadow diagonally from her feet. Behind her hangs a richly patterned carpet, with pale yellow-green leaves, lush flowers and coral pink vine tendrils signifying the hothouse femininity that the model embodies. As a fashion photograph it conveys the splendor of couture; but it lacks the vitality of much of Dahl-Wolfe's work. Many of her studio photographs display a similar bold use of lighting, and she often seems to be trying to re-create the effect of natural light, yearning to escape to the warm glow of the sun.

Her outdoor shots of New York fashions shimmer with a vitality that is missing from her more restrained interior shots. There also seems to be more distance placed between viewer and model, and this is perhaps to do with couture's exclusive nature, which seems to require a certain *gravitas* to its representation. In contrast, Dahl-Wolfe's invitingly constructed scenes of models tanning in the sun, wearing neat cotton separates that were within the reach of most, provide women with a fantasy of relaxation and pleasure in warmth and nature, rather than aspirational dreams of luxury and wealth.

During the 1930s and 1940s this seemed especially appealing: her pictures offered an American identity that was fashionable, but that women could relate to on their own terms. In a country founded on diverse groups of immigrants the representation of a coherent, easily-consumed—visually as well as literally—identity suggested a utopian ideal of stability. A designer's, photographer's or wearer's ability to project an American identity was more important than the reality of their origins. This *New York Times* headline of 1944 demonstrates the promise of integration and unity held out to immigrants: "Designer Stresses Outdoor Clothes—Joset Walker, Native of France, Described as Most American of our Stylists." (Pope 1944). The press coverage of Walker, a successful designer of "activewear" from the 1930s to the 1960s, continually emphasizes the Americanness of her work. In 1945 *The New York Sun* praises her use of the American pioneer woman as a source for her current collection, heralding "a return to the vigorous, young American spirit" (Chapman 1949).

Even though Walker frequently used diverse cultural references acquired in her travels to, for example, Guatemala and Vietnam in her designs, she maintained an American aesthetic that enabled women, and indeed the retailers who promoted her work, to relate to these cultures through assimilations of their own national identity. The simple forms she favored smoothed away differences and Americanized the body. Photographs of Lord and Taylor's window displays of Walker's Chinese-inspired collection of 1945 reinforce this. Mannequins are shown in various minimalist sets, dressed in simple Chinese-style jackets and "coolie" hats that offer the wearer the flavor of the Orient and the fantasy of travel without having to deviate from New York ready-to-wear's familiar signature style. During and just after the Second World War America was courting China as an ally, and various forms of propaganda were employed to promote this relationship to the American public. Walker's designs may not have been a deliberate part of this policy, but their presentation of key motifs of Chinese identity through the prism of American ideals promoted a sense of "visual colonialism." One outfit was described as "A slender dress inspired by Madame Chiang Kai-Shek . . . is a water green wool [and] . . . adapted to the American figure, will give the illusion that you're in China, especially if you pose flowers in your hair" (Blair 1945).

This opportunity to dress up while keeping a stable sense of American identity is strengthened by the idea of a single "American figure." While American women were as diverse as the clothing styles that were shown each season, it was a particular kind of New York-based ready-to-wear fashion and photographic representation that came to summarize America's fashion identity and, in contrast to the fantasies of Hollywood, a "realist" view of American femininity.

Martha Banta in her book *Imaging American Women, Ideas and Ideals in Cultural History* focuses on representations from the nineteenth century to the First World War, but her ideas are equally pertinent for the period under discussion. She states: "Unity within multiplicity was the cultural aim, but the cultural fact was multiplicity without unity" (Banta 1987: xxx). She goes on to show the role images play in propagating a myth of unified feminine identity: "Images of women were *created* as ideas not *found* as facts. At most, Americans took certain social facts and created ideas from them to suit their needs, not necessarily to report on their historical condition" (Banta 1987: xxxi).

Fashion photographs play a crucial role in this equation, since they enable women to visualize themselves as (white) Americans. Louise Dahl-Wolfe's photographs provide important examples of this process of "becoming" American, emphasizing qualities of naturalness, ease and lack of pretension that distinguish the American way of dressing from Parisian couture.

Nature

Two models rest on a jetty, looking out across the gray-blue water, their backs to the camera (Figure 3). One kneels next to the thick coiled rope of an anchor; she wears a vertically striped bathing costume by Louella Ballerino, its narrow straps extending between her shoulderblades. The other model stands, leaning against a piling at the edge of the water, her cotton summer dress blowing softly in the breeze. The fabric of the dress

Figure 3
Harper's Bazaar, May 1947.
Dress: Claire McCardell;
Swimsuit: for Jantzen by
Louella Ballerino. Photograph
by Louise Dahl-Wolfe.
Courtesy of The Museum of
the Fashion Institute of
Technology, New York.

is printed with subtly colored waves, which mimic the ripples on the water. Both are barefoot and casual; the colors of their clothes combine the brown tones of the wooden jetty and the dull brick red of the small boat moored at its side. The models seem absorbed in watching something out of view of the photograph, seemingly unaware that they are the subjects of our scrutiny. If it were not for the attention to detail and the careful composition, it could almost be a holiday snapshot. The picture, taken by Louise Dahl-Wolfe in 1947, emanates warmth, and as with so much of her work, seems to invite the viewer in. Although the models do not observe the viewer, the ease of their posture does not exclude or intimidate. They are at one with the natural surroundings; the subtle tones of the image look organic.

Martin Harrison has described Louise Dahl-Wolfe's work as "environmental" fashion photography (Harrison 1991: 88); and, as has already been shown in her photographs of American sportswear, there is a close relationship between model and habitat. While a student at the San Francisco Institute of Art, where she began her studies at the age of nineteen in 1914, Dahl-Wolfe was taught by Randolph Schaeffer, who pioneered teaching color theory at art schools. Schaeffer was inspired by the art historian Clive Bell, who "stressed that color is an inherent part of the expressive quality of form, and that color arrangements carry emotional weight, particularly brightly luminous colors which have a pleasing psychological effect" (Hall-Duncan 1979: 130). Dahl-Wolfe's color photography bears witness to this influence, using planes of color and light to create forms, and she seems especially adept at relating the tones of the skin and textiles to natural surroundings. While studying in San Francisco she had seen the 1915 World's Fair, and colors used by the Impressionist and Post-Impressionist paintings displayed there were to inspire her. She saw the Ballets Russes at around the same time, and was impressed by the dramatic use of color and sets designed by contemporary artists like Braque.

Her use of color enabled her to enrich her photographic vocabulary, and she was fastidious in her pursuit of high-resolution reproductions of her images, telephoning printers to ask about the quality of the paper they used to check on the clarity of color reproduction.

If color photography was one route to linking the body to nature, another was representation of nude or bathing suit-clad models against rippled sand dunes, blending the forms of the body with the curved forms etched in the sand. As a student she was introduced to the photographer Anne Brigman. Inspired by her soft-focused pictures of nudes, Dahl-Wolfe and her friends would pose naked for each other in the surrounding countryside, relating the shapes created by the body to nature and experimenting with light effects.

She continued her interest in the nude, influenced by her friend Edward Weston, whose own photographs of nudes on sand dunes from the mid-1930s were examinations of organic forms. Early in her career, Dahl-Wolfe had, like Weston, photographed still lifes of flowers and vegetables in black-and-white, studies of light and shade that emphasized the pure beauty of nature.

The relationship between body, nature and landscape constitutes a rich vein in American identity; the myth of the Edenic continent, extending to the mythological West: "From time immemorial the West had beckoned to statesmen and poets, existing as both a direction and a place, an imperialist theme and a pastoral Utopia" (Kitses 1970: 8).

In her focused images of models in generalized landscapes Dahl-Wolfe brought this dream of the open prairie to the fashion page. Other photographs speak directly of the agrarian West, like one of 1943 of Lauren Bacall in Claire McCardell cool cotton trousers and white blouse leaning against a paddock fence with a cow by her side. These photographs are visual statements of American identity. They lock into collective dreams of a vast continent. They appear to speak of "real" lives rather than fashion fantasies. During the war such photographs therefore provided an escape to an idyllic, calm countryside, as well as returning to the mythic image of woman and nature as one. They hinted at the return to this nurturing ideal once the war was over, tempering the practicality of the clothing with subconscious intimations of women's ultimate role in life.

City

Hand elegantly raised, fingers clasping a cigarette, the model poses for the camera. Her other hand rests on the balcony's rail, her neat black gloves signaling her respectability. She wears a small check tartan suit; the skirt is slightly flared and hangs in folds to the knee. The jacket is collarless and fitted close to her body; its shoulders are wide, broadening her frame and creating a bold silhouette; the jacket's edge is marked with large, raised metal buttons that pick up the light. Her hair is slicked back, barely visible beneath the quirky black hat that perches on the side of her head, topped with a double roll of fabric. She wears black high-heeled shoes; each adorned with a little bow. Her outfit is businesslike yet witty, the masculine swagger of her jacket tempered by discreet, feminine adornments. Her stance is poised and self-conscious: she is aware of her status as model, positioned to display and to be seen. She stands on the Museum of Modern Art in New York's starkly modernist balcony, leaning against its twin tubular rails. She is framed above by a white ceiling that is punctuated by a large circular hole that opens out to the skyline above. Her body appears hemmed in by the skyscrapers that loom in the mist behind her.

This photograph, taken in 1940 by Louise Dahl-Wolfe, depicts the model as a metropolitan woman. She is chic and controlled, dressed for the office or a meeting. Her pose is confident, yet she appears detached; she inhabits the city, yet she is dwarfed by it. Her feminine curves present a counterpoint to the graphic geometric lines of the modernist buildings that surround her. The checks on her suit are a witty imitation of the innumerable rectangular windows that puncture the high rises in the background, but the connection remains at the level of a visual pun. The setting does not relate to the model's body, as in Dahl-Wolfe's photographs of women and nature, but rather constructs a dramatic contrast to her form.

It is interesting to compare this image with a photograph from 1941 by Edward Weston. It shows David H. McAlpin, an investment banker and amateur photographer, who provided funds to support photography at the Museum of Modern Art and became the first chairman of the Committee on Photography at the Museum. McAlpin is also shown on a balcony, but this time it presents an anonymous corner, its rail creating a strident diagonal reaching back from the center of the photograph, rather than constructing a surrounding space that demarcates and encloses the body. His stance is dominant: his body side-on to the camera; one leg bent at the knee and thrust forward with his foot resting on the edge of the balcony. His torso also pushes into space, his head leant over the rail, chin resting in his cupped hand. He seems undisturbed by the photographer's presence, as he stares at the buildings opposite. Behind him the skyline is open; there are buildings all around him, but his image is pre-eminent; the balcony he stands on is level with several of the other structures, which makes him seem an equal to the city's might. He wears a dark suit; his shirt is barely visible, reduced to a clipped white edge at his neck. He is shown as dynamic and thoughtful, his presence dominating the space around him; he is at one with the modern metropolis. As a financier he is part of the capitalist heart of New York, and as a patron of the Museum of Modern Art, he is helping to shape the city's place at the forefront of modernism.

Since the nineteenth century "America [had] meant modernization" (Hartley 2000: 2), and the city was the locus of this progressive attitude. The city's constantly moving networks of people and power and its complex of thrusting, modernist architecture held out the promise of the future. Neil Campbell and Alasdair Kean wrote that "The very act of movement is akin to the desire for renewal, for 'becoming' American" (Campbell and Kean 1997: 34).

The link between movement, renewal and modernization is clear in *Harper's Bazaar*'s dynamic layout of the 1930s and 1940s. Alexey Brodovitch paced the magazine like a film, staging the photographs and white space to produce a rhythm that carried the reader through its pages, moving more quickly through a series of longer-range images, for example, before being slowed down by a close-up, more detailed photograph. The photographers that Brodovitch favored combined the current "realist" style of documentary photography, in blurred backgrounds signifying movement and change, with American fashion's pared-down forms.

During the inter-war period a loose group of New York-based photographers, dubbed "the New York School" by Jane Livingston in her 1992 book of the same title, sought to bring a new, candid style to their work. Image-makers like Weegee, Robert Frank and Saul Leiter espoused "a strong adherence to an idea of continual self-creation, and a quality of wanting to be responsible for one's own identity, one's own reality" (Livingston 1992: 259).

While *Harper's Bazaar* represented the commercial end of this ideal, Brodovitch and the students he taught at the New School of Social Research were also influenced by the desire to create photographs that "would express a quick charged *presentness*, and by so doing . . . move beyond what had already been done in the medium" (1992: 260). Thus fashion photographers like Munkacsi in the 1930s and Richard Avedon from the 1940s onwards strove to convey an instant in their work, and helped to reinforce the link between America, movement and modernity.

During the Second World War Brodovitch's style became more minimalist. New York fashion grew more confident and independent as it took center stage in the absence of Parisian influence. The clean layouts and pared-down photographic style fitted well with the functional fashions that were popular. By the time restrictions on fabric use were introduced under the L-85 scheme in 1943, many New York designers were already showing slim-line silhouettes that required a minimum of fabric. Examples of Claire McCardell's work in the Fashion Institute of Technology in New York's collection bear out this trend towards simple forms and utilitarian fabrics. A grey marl activewear set of c.1944 (76.33.7A/B), labeled "Claire McCardell clothes by Townley" is composed of a jersey hooded top, cut to fit and curve into the waistline. The matching flannel culottes are equally practical. The overall effect of the outfit is very streamlined and modernist. Although the top is cut to fit the woman's body, the ensemble produces a fairly androgynous figure, with the body seeming quite contained and protected by the soft fabric, which would have allowed the wearer to move about unhindered.

Such clothes hinted at more independence for women, and, combined with Brodovitch's stripped-down art direction and photographic style, "played a role in the transformation of fashion from an essentially aristocratic enterprise devoted to clothes manufactured in Paris into a broad-based (if no less narcissistic and hierarchical) preoccupation with personal and cultural 'lifestyles'" (Grundberg 1989: 19).

This focus on lifestyle was perfectly expressed in Louise Dahl-Wolfe's photographs, which were in tune with the active image of New York fashion. During the war, though, Dahl-Wolfe also produced images that promoted women's role in the war effort. Although two-thirds of American women remained within the home, there was a greater sense of opportunity for women to enter the workplace, and many took over jobs previously reserved for men. However, from the start there was an implicit time-limit on this increased opportunity, as it was only to be "for the duration." Fashion and glamor were linked to work in order to lure women into the workplace, with factories like the Lockheed Aircraft Plant holding fashion shows during lunch-hours. This also served to reinforce the notion that such spectacles were women's "natural" realm, to which they would return after the war.

Two of Louise Dahl-Wolfe's photographs from this period demonstrate the conflicting images of women presented in the 1940s. One from 1942 entitled "Keep the Home Fires Burning" shows a model with her back to the camera, kneeling before a blazing open fire in a comfortable sitting-room. She wears only a delicate, short slip. The bodice is of transparent lace, which is also used to trim its silk skirt. The model's lustrous hair is left loose, flowing down her back in soft curls. In contrast to this provocative image of a woman waiting patiently for her soldier husband to return, is a photograph of 1943 called "Goodbye to all that." In this image the model is shown first as a ghostly figure in what looks like a white Victorian nightgown, who stares benignly down from a spiral staircase. Beneath her is another more solid vision of the same model dressed in the military chic of a crisp white Wave uniform. This figure is turning back towards the other, out-of-date image of herself; she raises her hand, partly in farewell, partly beckoning the other, as a stand-in for the female viewer of the photograph, to join her in her new, active lifestyle. Women were therefore shown as both active workers and domesticated nurturers during the 1940s, and as William H. Chafe indicated, these ideas were frequently combined in the same image: "If a woman worked in a secretarial position, she was described as nurturant and 'wifely' in the way she took care of her boss . . . But whether the stereotype invoked was physical or emotional, reliance on such traditional images said a great deal about the difficulty of changing fundamental assumptions about sex roles" (Chafe 1991: 124).

Looking American

Louise Dahl-Wolfe was one of *Harper's Bazaar's* most prolific female fashion photographers. Her work during the 1930s and 1940s provided women experiencing the hardships of the Depression and the uncertainties of war with a means of visual escape. The escape her images offered seemed more "real" to many of *Harper's Bazaar's* readers than more avant-garde fashion imagery, since her photographs, provided scenes of warmth and light that welcomed the viewer in and were therefore especially effective when depicting New York fashion's easy-to-wear, relaxed styles. Dahl-Wolfe's photographs, as part of wider visual and design culture, take part in the process of Americanization; they offer ideals of national identity that the viewer is invited to assimilate as part of her own identity. By turns natural, healthy, sporty and practical, her fashion photographs are templates of idealized American femininity.

Notes

1. This article is based on preliminary research for the book, *American Looks, Women, Fashion and Modernity in New York, 1930–1960,* to be published in 2004 by I. B. Tauris. I am very grateful to the AHRB for providing funding to support this research as part of the "Fashion & Modernity" research group at Central Saint Martin's College of Art & Design, London.
2. Louise Dahl-Wolfe's memoirs, *A Photographer's Scrapbook,* St Martin's Press/Marek, 1984 and *Louise Dahl-Wolfe,* edited by Dorothy Twining Globus, Abrams, 2001, provide additional biographical details.

References

Banta, Martha. 1987. *Imaging American Women, Ideas and Ideals in Cultural History*. New York: Columbia University Press.

Blair, Beth. 1945. "Chinese Styles Make Spring Bid." *Peoria Morning Star*, 16 January.

Campbell, Neil and Alasdair Kean. 1997. *American Cultural Studies, An Introduction to American Culture*. London: Routledge.

Chafe, William H. 1991. *The Paradox of Change, American Women in the Twentieth Century*. New York: Oxford University Press.

Chapman, Georgia. 1949. "Lord and Taylor Resort Wear—1946 Styles Show Trend Toward Juvenile Motif." *The New York Sun*, 29 November.

Dahl-Wolfe, Louise. 1984. *A Photographer's Scrapbook*. New York: St Martin's/Marek.

Globus, Dorothy Twining (ed.). 2001. *Louise Dahl-Wolfe*. New York: Abrams.

Grundberg, Andy. 1989. *Brodovitch, Master of American Design*. New York: Harry N. Abrams.

Hall-Duncan, Nancy. 1979. *The History of Fashion Photography*. New York: Alpine Book Company Inc.

Harrison, Martin. 1991. *Appearances, Fashion Photography since 1945*. London: Jonathan Cape.

Hartley, John. 2000. "Introduction: 'Cultural Exceptionalism': Freedom, Imperialism, Power, America." In John Hartley and Roberta E. Pearson (eds), *American Cultural Studies, A Reader*. Oxford: Oxford University Press.

Kitses, Jim. 1970. *Horizons West*. London: Thames and Hudson/BFI.

Levine, Laurence W. 1988. "The Historian and the Icon: Photography and the History of the American People in the 1930s and 1940s." In Carl Fleischhauer and Beverley W. Brannan (eds), *Documenting America, 1935–1943*. Berkeley, CA: University of California Press.

Livingston, Jane. 1992. *The New York School, Photographs 1936–1963*. New York: Stewart Tabon & Chang.

Milbank, Caroline Rennolds. 1996. *New York Fashion, The Evolution of the American Look*. New York: Harry N. Abrams.

Polan, Dana. 1986. *Power and Paranoia, History, Narrative, and the American Cinema, 1940–1950*. New York: Columbia University Press.

Pope, Virginia. 1944. "Designer Stresses Outdoor Clothes—Joset Walker, Native of France, Described as Most American of our Stylists." *The New York Times*, 5 March.

Rowbotham, Sheila. 1999. *A Century of Women, The History of Women in Britain and the United States*. London: Penguin.

Fashion Theory, Volume 6, Issue 1, pp. 61–82
Reprints available directly from the Publishers.
Photocopying permitted by licence only.
© 2002 Berg. Printed in the United Kingdom.

The Politics of the First: The Emergence of the Black Model in the Civil Rights Era[1]

Janice Cheddie

Janice M. Cheddie is a Researcher in Visual Culture in the Historical and Cultural Studies Department, Goldsmiths College, University of London.

The oddest woman ever seen in fashion (or out of it for that matter) exploded into the glossy magazines in 1964.[2] Six foot tall, snarling, crouching, hands, crooked into claws, eyes rolling—this was Donyale Luna, the first black model to become an international star. She crashed through the color bar that, however, unwittingly had existed in the fashion business (Keenan 1977: 173).

There has been very little scholarly work that examines the entrance of the black woman into the mainstream Anglo-American fashion modeling industry. Within mainstream popular discourses, *if* black models are discussed at all, common-sense mythology is often reiterated: that black models appeared as a result of the growing liberalization of the fashion establishment, who belatedly acknowledged the beauty, grace and poise of black women·

As an illustration of fashion mythology I have drawn upon Brigid Keenan's popular work *The Women We Wanted To Look Like* (1976). While this work is extremely dated, it does locate and consolidate a number of themes that have developed concerning the entrance of the black model into the mainstream fashion industry, and that still resonate within contemporary fashion discourses: *the black model's poor ability to sell consumer goods, the narrative of the liberal progressive editor/ photographer, and the emergence of the anonymous glamorous black woman.*

Furthermore, Keenan's work is also of interest in that it is one of the few accounts that accurately cites the importance of Donyale Luna in the development of the black fashion model in Anglo-American fashion. In locating Luna *four* years before the emergence of Naomi Sims, who is often cited as the first black model to work within the mainstream Anglo-American fashion industry, we begin to see the emergence of a new historical trajectory in the history of the black model in the Anglo-American fashion industry and image.[3]

While it is common within black leisure magazines to have periodic features that demonstrate black women's struggle against racism and their triumph in being accepted within the mainstream fashion industry,[4] both black and mainstream popular accounts narrativize the emergence of black models as individual success stories divorced from their wider social and political contexts. In my analysis I am seeking to bring to the fore the wider social, political and economic context for the emergence of the black model. In doing so, I want to challenge the common-sense discourse of fashion mythology. Thus, it is my contention that within any analysis of the history of black models within the Anglo-American fashion industry and fashion image it is necessary to examine the intertextual relationship between *race, fashion and social protest.*[5]

Mainstream Fashion Mythology

It is important to dispel this fashion mythology precisely because fashion mythology locates a number of important factors that frame the emergence of the black model within the post-1945 Anglo-American fashion and advertising image, only to dismiss their wider social and cultural context.

The Black Model's Poor Ability to Sell Consumer Goods

Keenan's chapter "How Black Became Beautiful" argues that the lack of black women within the Anglo-American fashion industry was partly due to the perceived lack of economic buying power of the black consumer

(Keenan 1976: 173), rather than to institutionalize racism. Thus it is maintained that it was black models' inability to sell consumer goods that emerged as the key factor which stopped their appearance within Anglo-American fashion magazines, prior to the emergence of Luna in *Harper's Bazaar* in April 1965. While Keenan is correct in locating the development of the black consumer market in the US as an important marker in the emergence of the black model in the civil rights era, in my analysis, I wish to demonstrate that the economic power of the US black consumer was known to the fashion and advertising industries, *a decade* before Luna made her appearance.

The Narrative of the Liberal Progressive Editor/Photographer

Richard Avedon's decision to feature Luna in his April 1965 guest-edited edition of *Harper's Bazaar* is cited within fashion mythology as evidence of a liberal progressive editor moving things forward. Avedon's images of Luna not only reveal a moment in fashion history, but are also a pointer to a host of other histories and struggles—the history of the civil rights struggle to de-segregate advertising. In revealing this history I wish to challenge the common-sense assumption that black models appear as the result of a gradual liberalization of the attitudes of fashion editors and publishers, and demonstrate the direct pressure the civil rights leadership played in the appearance of the black model within mainstream advertising and fashion spreads (Applebaum 1964: 78). Luna's imaging also draws our attention to a number of contending discourses operating within the representation of the black woman in the civil rights era—discourses of primitivism and glamor.

The Emergence of the Anonymous Glamorous Black Woman

Luna's image highlights, not as Keenan claims, the discovery of the "fashion negress" (Keenan 1977: 173), but the importance of the emergence of the anonymous fashionable glamorous black woman within mainstream media representations. This image of black femininity, as I wish to demonstrate, was present in media representations prior to the emergence of Donyale Luna in 1965, and is an important precursor to the emergence of the black model within Anglo-American fashion magazines.

Race, Fashion and Black Femininity

The entrance of the black model into the fashion industry also highlights the need to address wider historical, aesthetic and social discourses concerning the historical exclusion of black women from mainstream Western discourses of beauty, femininity and attractiveness: and the assertion that black women could only be considered beautiful if they were light-skinned. While they form important framing discourses to the entrance of the black model into the fashion industry and discourses of femininity, a detailed analysis of these issues is beyond the scope of this article,[6] though it is interesting to note that the most successful and well-known black models in the twentieth century were dark-skinned women: Naomi Sims (late 1960s/1970s); Iman (1970s); and Naomi Campbell (1980s/1990s).

Within this article I wish to demonstrate that in order to locate the meaning and significance of Donyale Luna, we must first uncover the socio-cultural terrain that determined the emergence of the anonymous black woman in the desegregated fashion and advertising industries as a figure of glamor. Thus my primary focus is the social and historical context of the black model's emergence within the fashion industries rather than a semiotic analysis of their representations. Instead of reading the emergence of the black model as a symbolic representation of the civil rights struggle, it may be useful to conceptualize the presence of the black model as a "supplement":[7]

> . . . the supplement supplements. It adds only to replace. It intervenes or insinuates itself *in-the-place-of*: if it fills, it is as if one fills a void. If it represents and makes an image, it is by the anterior default of a presence. Compensatory and vicarious, the supplement is an adjunct, a subaltern which *takes (the) place*. As a substitute it is not simply added to the positivity of a presence; it produces no relief, its place is assigned in the structure by a mark of emptiness. Somewhere, something can be filled through sign and proxy (Derrida, quoted in Rogoff 2000: 56).

The black model within the civil rights fashion image operates within the tension between the cultural struggle for representation, civil rights, and democracy and the denial of that struggle. She operates not as symbolic representation of that struggle but rather sliding between symbolic representation and the political struggles of race, class and femininity.

In order to explore the social and cultural terrain of the 1950s and 1960s in the US I have sought to employ an intertextual analysis to examine the entrance of black women into the Anglo-American modeling profession and the ways in which the civil rights struggle affected the emergence and development of the black model. It is my assertion that it is only once this struggle has taken place that we witness the appearance of black models in US as well as British fashion magazines. Furthermore, I wish to demonstrate the ways in which an excavation of this hidden history also highlights the ways in which the discourses of the civil rights movement entered the codes and symbols of the everyday.

Secondly, this article seeks to explore the ways in which the US social, cultural and economic developments in the civil rights era opened up new cultural spaces that created a demand for a greater proliferation of images of black women as figures of glamor—cultural spaces that are foregrounded by the targeting and development of the "underdeveloped" expanding $15 billion black consumer market, which initially created a demand for black models within segregated advertising campaigns. For black discourses, however, the struggle for the desegregation of advertising and the emergence of the black model had a wider significance, because the emergence of black models encapsulates a number of themes within black bourgeois discourses on femininity: *reclaiming black beauty; adoption of the codes of bourgeois femininity; inclusiveness,* and *democracy.*

Thirdly, I wish to illustrate how the anonymous black woman as a figure of glamor was an important figure in the development of the black model. Black discourses positioned this image of black femininity as a literal embodiment of black demands for integration, progress and assimilation into the US mainstream. The representation of black femininity as glamorous, presents this bourgeois ideal of femininity as a symbol of racial inclusiveness, transforming the demands for civil rights into images of class homogeneity (Weigman 1991). However, Avedon's imaging of Luna alerts us to the perverseness of primitivism as an element in the discursive repertoire of mainstream representations of black women.

During the civil rights era the fashion industry was a site of conflicting and contradictory demands concerning the meaning and relevance of the black body. In order to understand how, within dominant representations, these forces converge and collide I believe it is useful to draw upon Stuart Hall's (1978) assertion that racism from previous historical periods can co-exist with new and emerging discourses about the concept and meanings of race. Within the representations of black models in the civil rights era, the black woman's body is both a site of inclusiveness, unthreatening and assimilated into the dominant discourses of feminine attractiveness (through the construction of the black woman as glamorous), and of the continuing portrayal of the black woman as primitive—a body valued for its "intensity of color"[8] and physicality. These two contending discourses are played out within the emergence of Beverley Valdes in 1962 and Luna 1965.

■ In 1962 Beverley Valdes was the first black model to work on Seventh Avenue, the home of the New York fashion and garment industry:

> Beverley Valdes 24. Willowy and exotic eyed, she was hired last year as the showroom model by prestigious designer Pauline Trigere. "Her interesting color looked well with the burnt oranges and greens that I was using" said Miss Trigere, who had interviewed 40 mostly white applicants before picking Beverley (*Newsweek* 1962: 69).

However, also present in the reporting of this highly publicized event are discourses of meritocracy—discourses that position Valdes as simply the best woman for the job—regardless of race, choosing to ignore the ways in which Valdes breaks the *de facto* segregation of the New

York fashion industry, while simultaneously attempting to deny the effects of the civil rights movement's pressure on all aspects of US civic life—including the New York fashion industry.

■ Secondly, within two of Avedon's six *Harper's Bazaar* photographs of Luna, she is imaged within the photographs and the accompanying text in ways that stress her exoticism and primitive sexuality. In Avedon's representations of Luna, Luna is being positioned as a signifier of "African" culture, rather than American culture:

> THE TALL STRENGTH and pride of movement of a Masai warrior: Donyale Luna, gauzed in silk (*Harper's Bazaar* 1965: 160).

In these two images Luna is also photographed in tiger and leopard prints, with her hands gesturing in a claw-like action in one image and on all fours in another. However, despite Keenan's assertion that Luna is represented as an outlandish figure styled to portray an animalistic, exotic woman, the overriding image Avedon presents within the fashion spread is of Luna as an elegant, glamorous black woman. This imaging of Luna draws upon modernity's imagining of the black body as a signifier, often simultaneously, of the modern (glamor) and the primitive (Clifford 1988: 168).

The Triumph of Bourgeois Femininity

Finally, I wish to argue that in the civil rights era there was a shift in the imagining of black femininity within the fashion arena from stereotypical representations to an image of black femininity as that of a woman of glamor, an image of femininity that is premised on the artificiality of its surface appearance (Kuhn 1986; Dyer 1992). Within this framework glamor, and by implication femininity and attractiveness, is a constructed image achieved through artifice rather than through being the possessor of a "natural" racially defined beauty—and thus a more inclusive category, transforming the notion of glamor from an exclusively white category to a signifier of a Westernized urban modernity.

Despite the continuing presence of primitivist imaging within the civil rights era, as demonstrated by some of Avedon's images of Luna, within 1950s black discourses the dominant image of femininity was the production of a black feminine corporeal style that stressed feminine concealment, understatement, discretion, and a concerted effort to counter charges of hypersexuality, "sexless elegance" (Wilson 1992: 34). While this period continues to see a predominance of light-skinned black women,[9] within the representation of the black woman as a figure of glamor,[10] beauty and desirability, this hegemony begins to break down in the 1950s: with the expansion of the black middle class, light-skinned-ness as a signifier of class and social position had begun to break down in the early part of the twentieth century (Franklin Fraser 1965; Carby 1987).

The breakdown of this hegemonic representation of black feminine beauty is illustrated by the success and prominence of the dark-skinned black model Helen Williams in black leisure magazines of the 1950s;[11] and also later by Naomi Sims, who gains international prominence and recognition within an integrated fashion industry in the late 1960s. In representations of Williams in the 1950s it is the image of black woman as a sophisticated woman of glamour that comes to the fore:[12] "A modern Nefertiti, she gave a cool-edged glamour to the image of warm, honey-colored women . . . Helen was a cameo of sophisticated serenity. Her versatility sold products from clothes and cosmetics to alcohol, often in the sepia version of white ads" (Summers 1987: 40). The image of the black woman as a figure of glamor, as it emerged within the civil rights era, was a representation that was appealing to black and white commentators because it is an image that champions the bourgeois ideal of femininity—an image of beauty that was achieved in the 1950s through commodity consumption and poise. This image has had very different meanings within black and white discourses.

1944–1954: *Ebony* Magazine and the Identification of the Black Consumer Market, and the Development of Segregated Advertising

The civil rights era in the US saw the flowering of black-owned and controlled magazines and newspapers catering to and for the expanding black middle class, providing for the first time a marketing opportunity for white advertisers to address directly black readers and consumers in a leisure-orientated format.

In 1945 *Ebony* was launched and quickly established and promoted itself as the first and largest mass-circulation black-owned "entertainment-oriented" magazine. *Ebony* imitated the highly successful photo journal *Life* magazine, establishing itself as the voice of the black middle class (Daniels 1982). Six months after the launch of *Ebony*, its publishers the Johnson Publishing Company (JPC) began to approach mainstream advertisers to place adverts within *Ebony*. In an effort to persuade the mainstream of the value of the black consumer, in 1952 the head of JPC published an article in the advertising journal *Advertising Age* claiming that "the Black consumer market—which even in that era of suffocating segregation had $15 billion worth of buying power—was 'ripe and ready' for market exploitation" (*Ebony* 1992: 60).

After identifying the size and buying power of the black consumer market, JPC set about changing white advertising companies' marketing strategies directed at the black consumer. JPC argued that "Black Americans, like any other consumer group, would be more receptive to advertisements featuring models with whom they as black people could identify" (*Ebony* 1992: 60)—and that black consumers could not identify with racist stereotypes. The JPC sales team persuaded some mainstream advertisers to run parallel ads in *Ebony* and *Life* magazine with the advertisers using black models in *Ebony* and white models in *Life*.

The adverts featuring black models, portrayed in identical ways to their white counterparts, tested better with black consumers. This led initially to duplicate segregated advertisements, where black models appeared *only* in black magazines promoting the same products, using the same sets and props as their white counterparts who appeared in the more lucrative mainstream/national campaigns. However, the targeting of black consumers by mainstream advertisements led directly to the opening up of modeling as a career option for young black women and the development of an infrastructure where black women could train and find work as professional models through legitimate formalized structures (*Ebony* 1992: 60).

From "Mammy" to Black Model

The establishment of a segregated advertising industry was a crucial development that led to the identification of a need and demand for black models to sell products to black consumers. These developments led to a change in the methods used to target the expanding black consumer market, and was a precursor to the entry of the black woman into the modeling industry as a figure of glamor. *The New York Post*, in June 1955, reported on the changing image of the black woman from "mammy" to glamorous model, linking this changing image to the "discovery" of the lucrative black market, which did not respond positively towards products that used in their advertising images racist representations of black people.

Once the segregated advertising market had established that anonymous black women could feature as glamorous figures to sell consumer goods the struggle defined by the black press and the civil rights leadership was to have black models featured in desegregated national and local advertising. However, despite a series of breakthroughs, progress towards full integration was painfully slow. The narrowness of the segregated advertising and fashion market meant that black models in this period remained in a precarious and marginalized economic position (*Ebony* 1954: 100).

Jobs for black models in integrated firms in the period 1944–1954 were largely one-offs and sporadic appearances, with the models continuing to find their careers hampered by prejudice and stereotyping:

> We've had girls from here take showroom jobs on Seventh Av. and they only last a couple of days there. The clients claim they get complaints from their customers and that Southern buyers don't

> approve of Negro girls being displayed in the showroom. And the department stores won't accept us either. They always say we're too short or too fat or too skinny (*New York Post* 1955: 30).

In spite of the prejudice of white employers and their clients, opportunities in integrated companies were sought after, because they represented the potential for black models to break out of the limited black consumer market and into the more lucrative and potentially economically secure mainstream market.

The Black Model as a Signifier of Democracy

At the beginning of the 1960s the civil rights leadership sought proactively to desegregate the advertising industry by asking major corporations and department stores to use black models in their advertising. In 1963, in an attempt to tackle the reluctance of advertisers to use black models more extensively in their national campaigns, the civil rights leadership met with the major advertising companies to discuss the issue of segregation in national advertising. The outcome of the meeting was to be the greater use of black models in integrated advertising campaigns (*Newsweek* 1963: 68).

By 1963 advertisers also came under severe pressure from the US government through the Warner Committee, who, finding only "two integrated ads in the editions of four major magazines, reported last week that 26 companies (including IBM, Northrop, RCA, Equitable Life & Royal McBee) have used Negro models in national media this year while 20 others . . . have issued firm commitments" (*Newsweek* 1963: 68). However, many advertisers continued to resist the idea of using black models, arguing that black women were outside the dominant notions of beauty and attractiveness: "One Detroit auto official snaps 'We don't hire Negro models. We also don't hire fat models. When you have a pretty car, you want to dress it up to the best advantage, so you get the best looking girl you can to go with it'" (*Newsweek* 1963: 68). The major push to use black models came in 1968 after the New York Commission on Human Rights, which dealt directly with the employment of blacks in advertising and broadcasting, and the death of Martin Luther King Jnr. It is against this background that we see the rise to prominence of Naomi Sims within integrated American and international fashion.

Black Magazines: Discourses of Bourgeois Femininity

While the themes of integration and inclusiveness informed and constructed the struggle over the meaning and significance of the black presence within previously racially segregated spaces, in the civil rights era the meaning attached to the emergence of the black model was also a contested site in black and white discourses. Within white discourses the emergence of black models was not positioned as a result of pressure from the civil rights movement—but as a market response to the growing black consumer market.

However, the black leisure magazines failed to address the central issue of why black women were excluded from dominant definitions of beauty and attractiveness, and the identification of black women's sexuality with the primitive and the promiscuous. Rather, what the language used within magazines of this period seeks to do is to code these issues within a language of acceptance of the dominant definitions, not to change or challenge these discourses, but rather to make them more inclusive; and also to demonstrate that black women were *worthy* enough to be included within these categories:

> The face and body (almost all of it) of a lovely young Negro woman appears between the covers of a national magazine. College kids vote Negro beauties high honors as homecoming queens. Increasingly Negro girls are winning integrated beauty contests. Slowly but surely the faces and figures are being recognized as assets in the advertising and fashion fields . . .
>
> *Negro enrolment in charm schools is skyrocketing. Not infrequently, Negro writers describe Negro women as beautiful.* No longer is Lena Horne or Dorothy Dandridge viewed "as an exception to the rule." All of this, and more, illustrates America's latest discovery, the beauty in Negro women (Young 1963: 42) (emphasis added).

It is this emphasis within black discourse that placed such a high premium on the adoption of the codes and attire of bourgeois femininity. Direct and open challenges to eurocentric notions of beauty and attractiveness come only with the emergence of the counter-hegemonic discourses of black cultural nationalism in the late 1960s, and are not expressed within the bourgeois discourses of the black leisure magazines of the 1950s and 1960s.[13]

In order to understand the significance of the emergence of the black model to discourses concerning black femininity I am seeking to examine the dominant discourses of femininity within the black leisure-orientated magazines of the civil rights era, precisely because it was this readership at which the segregated advertising campaigns were aimed. Furthermore, the magazines themselves sought to establish themselves as the voice of the urban sophisticated middle class; and within the discourses of the urban black middle class the image of the glamorous black woman is an image that is seen by these discourses to embody the translation of black middle-class desires for racial equality into middle-class success and aspiration.

Reclaiming Black Beauty

The way in which the underlying theme of the racist nature of eurocentric discourses on black femininity and attractiveness is dealt with in black leisure magazines of the period is through concepts of respect, self-worth and self-reliance. Within the articulation of these concepts the emphasis is on the behavior and attire of the individual black woman. Thus, the dominant theme within black magazines of the civil rights era was the reclamation of black femininity from racist discourses, which sought to position the black woman as outside the dominant ideals of "respectable" femininity and attractiveness. Black entertainment and leisure magazines of the civil rights era sought to reclaim black femininity by proclaiming the black woman's beauty and respectability, characteristics that had been denied to her by the legacy of slavery.[14]

The themes of respect and recognition for the black woman's beauty and desirability are articulated in A. S. "Doc" Young's article "Beauty In Negro Women".[15] Writing about the new-found recognition of beauty in black women illustrated, for Young, by the use of black models in previously segregated arenas, he states that: "The word 'respect' is important here. The fact is that throughout history the Negro woman has been sought after. But this seeking hasn't always been complimentary. Today, however the Negro woman realizes the value of her beauty more than any of her predecessors. She commands respect and gets it" (Young 1963: 43). Black writers of the civil rights era also identified a hunger and a desire in black audiences to see black women in glamorous and fashionable roles—not just as noble and long-suffering heroic women. These writers maintained that as a result of portraying the black woman as a heroic figure black women were disenfranchised from the dominant discourses of femininity, which proclaimed that women should be weak, passive and dependent—not heroic and strong, which were masculine traits, thus denying black women their femininity (Young 1963). In this quest to establish within white society the idea of the beautiful black woman, black magazines saw the black model as important in the development of the belief that black women were beautiful and desirable women as defined by the dominant discourses of 1950s femininity.

Codes of Femininity

In representations of the black female body, black magazines sought to represent a black female body that aspired to be included within the white-dominated ideals of beauty, femininity and respectability. For black magazines of the period this desired respectability and recognition for the black woman was achieved through the presentation of the black female body, a body that aims to play down and conceal racial difference through the adoption of a bourgeois dress code, a symbol, for black magazines of the period, of respectable bourgeois femininity.

This struggle for acceptance is for black magazines a two-way process. Firstly, black magazines sought to challenge the racist denial of black women's beauty and attractiveness. Within these discourses we see concepts of racial progress being translated into discourse of individual class aspiration, taste and demeanor. In this way, the bourgeois ideal of femininity is held out as an all-inclusive category. It is against this discursive framework that we can begin to understand the motivation behind the assertion that black women should adopt more conservative attire. The most blatant example of this is an article, published in June 1954 by *Jet*,[16] a black entertainment magazine, asking its readers the question "Do Negro Women Overdress?" While this is an overt illustration of this bourgeois discourse, I believe that the article's underlying assumptions framed the ways in which issues concerning black femininity and its representation are presented within black leisure magazines of the 1950s. Furthermore, this discourse and the emergence of an initially segregated advertising market fueled the demand for the black model as a glamorous bourgeois woman.

"Do Negro Women Overdress" details the observations of a visiting dignitary from the Midwest to a Southern church, who states that "southern churches and schoolrooms housed the most overdressed women in the nation" (*Jet* 1954: 40). This article makes overt the discourses that the black leisure magazines of the civil rights era were seeking to project and the driving motivation behind this discourse—namely to demonstrate to white society that black women were not gaudy,[17] overdressed, sexually deviant women—rather than rejecting the condemnation of black women as "overdressed" as a racist accusation based on the assertion that black women were ostentatious and gaudy, and incapable of coming to grips with the bourgeois feminine dress code. The article never raises the question of who defines "overdressing": rather the article accepts the accusation as "true" and attempts to counteract the accusation by claiming that black women have adopted a more conservative style and learnt how to select the "'correct attire' designed for her figure, age and her profession" (*Jet* 1954: 42). On the basis of its uncritical acceptance of bourgeois ideals of feminine display, *Jet* states to its readers that while accusations of overdressing may have been true in the past, black women are now more in step with the norms and codes of bourgeois feminine display. Furthermore, black women have taken these lessons to heart and overcome the difficulties in getting cosmetics in a consumer market that did not cater to their specific needs: "'We have become more conservative and tend to bypass loud colors and styles and unbecoming styles we once favored. On the whole, we have solved our special problem of selecting colors to complement our particular complexions and are toning down the flamboyance of which we are often accused': L'Tanya, Fashion Designer" (*Jet* 1954: 41).

Inscribed throughout the article are issues related to notions of class and taste. *Jet*, in engaging with this racist assumption concerning black women's sexuality and dress, seeks to signal to its sophisticated urban Northern readership that, if they had been guilty of these sins, they too could now adopt a discreet, elegant feminine style. Thus, *Jet* advises its black women readers: "After you get dressed, take off half the jewelry, feathers, flowers and bows you have managed to stick on yourself" (*Jet* 1954: 41). The article demonstrates to its readers how to master the dominant codes of bourgeois feminine display in an effort to conform to the social dress rules and codes of white middle-class America, codes that stressed feminine "understatement" and "concealment," and a style that is above all respectable and plays down overt displays of sexuality.

Therefore *Jet* is proud to announce that black women are learning to master the correct rules of bourgeois femininity:

> Our women are mastering all the tricks of timing and restraint, of selecting the proper attire for the time of the day and clothes that have that quiet elegant look: Ruth Ellington (*Jet* 1954: 41).

> On the whole Negro women are not flagrantly guilty of over-dressing, but there are still some who fancy heavily-beaded suits, cocktail dresses in the morning and clustered jewelry at high noon (*Jet* 1954: 42).

The translation of racial pride into class aspiration is marked upon the black woman's body. For these writers of the civil rights period the professional career black woman represented a woman who was able to master her body through choosing clothes that were "suitable" for her individual needs. Within the image of the black female professional we are presented with a feminine dress style that attempts to tone down the markers of racial difference by adopting the formal sartorial code of the professional white middle-class woman:

> Chicago's Edith Sampson, former United Nations representative . . . laughingly recalls: "Once I considered myself well dressed when my taffeta frock rustled, birds and feathers flew from my hat, minks swathed my shoulders and satin pumps glistened on my feet." Today she considers herself well dressed when attired in handsomely-tailored suits and unpretentious dresses especially designed for her figure, age and her profession as an attorney (*Jet* 1954: 42).

For black magazines that emerged in the civil rights era the aspirational figure of the black professional career woman was championed precisely because she represented a black woman who had successfully mastered this translation of racial progress into middle-class aspiration *within* the dominant codes of femininity and attractiveness.

It was against this background of championing new models of black femininity that Helen Williams was seen as a symbol of the emerging black femininity. The imaging of Williams in the civil rights era visually demonstrated to the readers of the black leisure magazines the new model of black femininity the magazines sought to promote—cool, sophisticated, bourgeois, urban and glamorous. Thus, the emergence of the black model in mainstream magazines was seen not only as a signifier of black women being accepted as attractive but also as a signifier of black women learning the codes and symbols of bourgeois femininity, a key marker within the discourses of the black leisure magazines of the period of black women's ability to win acceptance within the mainstream. This figure of the elegant glamorous black woman crosses over into mainstream fashion through the image of Sims, who, unlike Luna, is not an outlandish figure but a woman who has mastered the codes of discreet bourgeois feminine display:

> . . . in 1969 *Life* magazine[18] were able to put Naomi Sims on their cover with two words "Top Model." This lady was not called upon to growl, crawl or crouch, she was accepted for what she was, a beautiful elegant woman who happened to be black. She has been on the best-dressed list several years running, she wears no freaky clothes but dresses simply in pastel colors or white. She does her hair in a refined version of the Afro and her make-up is natural— no day-glo turquoise on her lids or pale pink on her lips, but a subtle blend of highlights and dark shadows and brown-red lipstick (Keenan 1977: 178).

Proximity to Whiteness?

Common-sense discourses concerning the predominance of light-skinned black models in mainstream magazines locate the reason for the over-use of the light-skinned black woman as being due to the light-skinned black woman's alleged proximity to whiteness. In her autobiography Sims reiterates this assertion (Sims 1979: 154). However, I wish to argue that the emergence of the black model within the civil rights era challenges this premise. For it is within the civil rights era that we first witness the use of black models *because of* their racial identity. The model Jane Hoffman sums up the common-sense history of black models in the civil rights era:

> First there was the Negro that looked white. She soothed the company's conscience. They'd say "We used a Negro." Yeah? Where? Then there was the Negro girl you'd think of as something else. She wasn't even beautiful—just a weird creature, some kind of space thing. She had to be so bizarre that no one could identify with her. I had people turn me down saying "Oh Jane! You're too beautiful!" Now they'll say you're not Negro enough! Such ironies

are rather a bitter truth for black models who range in skin color from *café au lait* to very black (*Ebony* 1970: 159).

However, black models during the civil rights era had to be perceived by white audiences as "black," but not so dark as to offend white notions that beauty in black women only resides in light-skinned black women. Thus in the civil rights era we see the black model's ability to signify blackness emerge as *one* of the key elements that decided whether or not a black model worked in mainstream fashion spreads and advertising images. During this period black models argue that fashion employers rejected in their fashion spreads and advertising images black women with hair, skin and physical features they did not immediately identify as being black: "Lucielle Rich who is 23 and stunningly pretty often finds her fair skin a disadvantage. 'I've been told by clients I'm too fair for the typical Negroid type, but I don't think there is a typical Negroid type. They'll call the agency and say "Send us a girl we know is colored".'" (*New York Post* 1955: 30).

In analyzing the presence of the light-skinned black model, Derrida's notion of a "supplement" comes into play. Within mainstream cultural spaces the model's presence is an adjunct, not a symbolic marker of the struggle for civil rights. Rather, the light-skinned black model's presence offers no relief, for it operates both to signify a black presence and also to negate that presence. Conceptualizing the model's presence as a "supplement" suggests that the struggles, anticipation, fears and desires are not simply derived from the discursive sphere of the civil rights movement but are actually interwoven into the fabric of representation. The light-skinned black model operates within mainstream cultural spaces as a body that plays down "difference," while her presence is coded within the photographic aesthetics (lighting, make-up, clothes, props, etc.) of mainstream 1950s advertising as a "simulacrum" of the white model. Thus the light-skinned black model within these spaces fails to fulfill the desire for a black presence, while simultaneously occupying the sign of "whiteness," that is her presence is transformed into the commodification of feminine beauty to sell consumer goods. However, the light-skinned black model's presence is not to signify "whiteness" as the common-sense discourses assert; rather she operates within mainstream fashion as a mark of emptiness, a void rather than a symbolic representation of the civil rights struggle.

Limited Breakthroughs

Despite the breakthroughs for black models at the beginning of the 1960s the lucrative and socially prestigious high-fashion magazines *Vogue* and *Harper's Bazaar* had not featured a black model within their pages: "Light or dark no Negroes have successfully stormed the citadels of high fashion,

Vogue & Harper's Bazaar. "If the right situation came up we would certainly use some of the Negroes in our files" insists a Vogue model editor (*Newsweek* 1963: 69), maintaining in 1962 that it was not institutionalized racism that was stopping *Vogue* using black models, but rather that "the right situation" had not occurred. These comments suggest that the editor of *Vogue* had no influence or control in creating the situation where a black model might be used. Rather *Vogue* leads us to the conclusion that black models were not being judged on their ability as models or by their ability to reflect the ideals of beauty and femininity, but rather that there were a number of external factors that is contemporary racial politics, that governed their appearance in mainstream magazines.

The significance of Donyale Luna is not her role in desegregating the mainstream fashion image, but rather her ability to break through into the top-earning field of high-fashion magazines, modeling and advertising work. It is in this sense that Luna is cited by Sims in *Ebony* May 1970 as paving the way for models such as herself in this lucrative arena.

Luna achieves a "first" in that she breaks the segregation of one of the most prestigious arenas of fashion modeling, *Harper's Bazaar*. However, by the time Luna appears in the pages of Avedon's April 1965 edition of *Harper's Bazaar*, her presence is not greeted with any fanfare or celebration in the black press. Luna merely becomes another first in the history of fashion modeling, in an era of "firsts."[19]

Meanwhile, the representation of the black woman as a signifier of the animalistic and primitive continues to be a constant frame of reference in high-fashion magazines. This primitivism is negotiated through the codes and motifs of high fashion and popular music. This tension between the exotic primitive and the bourgeois woman continues to resonate throughout mainstream fashion. An examination of British model Naomi Campbell's career in the 1980s and 1990s witnesses her success in straddling the two demands for the bourgeois woman and for the exotic primitive.

The representation of black femininity that emerges within the fashion image in the civil rights era is the image of the bourgeois, glamorous black woman, an image that is also mirrored by the success of the female African American group the Supremes within this period.[20] The shift in representations from exotic primitive to black woman of glamor in the fashion image is confirmed when by the end of the 1960s the most successful image of black femininity is glamorous dark-skinned Sims. Descriptions of Sims are dominated by her "class" and "breeding" and "control" of her image:

> HERS IS THE BEAUTY of the thoroughbred, it occurred to this writer while watching the Derby a few days after he interviewed Naomi Sims . . . clean head, the slimness, the height, the legs. And most of all class. It has made her one of the five top fashion models in the world, the other four are white. Now she sat on one of the

> black floor pillows of her . . . 70s apartment, her dark brown self
> set off against a white sweater and pants, two white ivory bracelets—
> one of them a thin white disc—and cherry colored clogs. It is as
> though she were always in a certain pool of quiet thought; a private
> pool. She is an appraiser, once having appraised, she talks, direct,
> informative interesting (*New York Post* 1972: 32).

Framed by the civil rights discourse, Sims' image is read by black commentators as a positive image for black women. In her professional career Sims quickly gained a reputation of being a controlled, sophisticated beauty actively resisting the image of the black woman as "sexual primitive." She attempted to do this by projecting an image of black femininity that is premised on sexless elegance and regality: "Nothing was too good for a picture . . . the editors would call for more fantasy. I gave them elegance and regality. We were reaching for the stars." (quoted in Summers 1987: 41).

Sims stands out in the history of black models—not only because she was the first to break into the lucrative arena of high-fashion modeling, but also because her presence as a highly successful dark-skinned black woman in the fashion arena was read by black readers in particular as a direct response to the slogan "Black Is Beautiful." Sims' image became an image that many black women could and would identify with (Summers 1987: 41).

The lasting image of Sims as a glamorous black woman is an image of black femininity as power, control and glamor—an image of black femininity that exists as a form of closure, a sealing off of black female sexuality as inviting, thus establishing within the fashion industry the image of the black woman as the possessor of an aloof and seemingly unattainable sexuality, in line with mainstream Western fashion represent-ations of female sexuality.

Acknowledgments

Thanks to Sue Thornham and Deborah Thomas, University of Sunderland, Richard Dyer, and the Willie Family, Brooklyn, New York.

Notes

1. In my analysis I am using the term "civil rights era" to position a discursive repertoire that framed the meaning and understanding of the black struggle for racial equality in America. Rather than focusing on the boundaries set by strict historical dates, I have focused my analysis on how the discursive repertoire of the civil rights movement

provided a framework for discussions around race, democracy and citizenship. It is my assertion that the discourses of the civil rights era did not begin in 1954 and end in 1965, but rather that they moved from being the dominant discourses in the post-1945 era that set the parameters in discussions around race, democracy and citizenship to being one of a number of discourses mobilized in the struggle against racial inequality in the late twentieth century.

2. Keenan is incorrect in citing this date. Luna appears in Richard Avedon's guest-edited edition of *Harper's Bazaar* in April 1965.

3. I am using the term Anglo-American specifically, as the history of black models in continental Europe has been very different—but is likewise very poorly researched.

4. For an example of this see Summers (1987).

5. I would also add music to this list; this article does not touch upon the influence of popular culture on the fashion image.

6. These issues have been dealt with in Honor (1989), Bush (1981) and hooks (1986), who bluntly state the division within dominant black discourses on femininity:

> In the black community the fair skinned black woman who nearly reassembled the white woman was seen as the "lady" and placed on a pedestal while the darker skinned women were seen as bitches and whores. (hooks: 1986: 110).

7. I have taken this use of the supplement from Rogoff (2000: 56).

8. The use of black skin for European perceptions of its ability to "show off" color is discussed in Honor (1989) and Dabydeen (1987).

9. Richard Dyer, in his study of Paul Robeson in *Heavenly Bodies* (1982) reminds us that while white society has been willing to accept dark-skinned black men in public life, it has only accepted black women as beautiful if they were light-skinned. This definition of beauty excludes the majority of black women and denies the range and diversity of black women's beauty. "It was the lot of black women stars to become known for their beauty only to the degree that they are fair" (Dyer 1982: 114).

10. This shift has been discussed at length in relationship to cinematic representations by Bogle (1980).

11. Williams, like another dark-skinned black model Naomi Sims, who was to be the first black millionairess model, was also turned down by Eileen Ford of the Top US agency Ford Model Inc. (Summers 1987).

12. Furthermore Williams's image in this period is remarkably similar in some ways to representations of the film star Lena Horne in the 1940s (see Bogle 1980).

13. Black fashion and beauty pageants with an emphasis on Afro-centric beauty were started in the 1950s (see Toure 1971); the most well-known ones were the Naturally fashion shows that began in New York in the 1950s.

14. "The red stain of bastardy which two centuries of systematic legal defilement of Negro women had stamped upon his race, meant not only the loss of ancient African chastity, but also the hereditary weight of mass corruption from white adulterers threatening almost the obliteration of the Negro home" (Du Bois 1982 [1902]: 50).
15. *Sepia*, September 1963. *Sepia*, founded in 1947, like the black magazine *Ebony* is a successful photojournal which has been able through the use of good photography and layout to attract advertisers and a large readership. "Like most other black periodicals, *Sepia* emphasises achievement within the race. . . . *Sepia*, however, remains basically a newspaper with a focus on black achievement" (Daniels, 1982: p. 345).
16. *Jet*, a pocket-sized magazine, was first published in October 1951. It had in most of its issues a centrefold black bathing beauty. "The format includes a few in-depth news stories. Most of the content is distributed among business, education, religion, health, medicine, journalism, politics. labor, poverty and crime sections" (Daniels 1982: 213–14).
17. A common belief that emerged during slavery was that black women had an excessive fondness for "loud" colors, and hooks (1986) argues that black women sought through clothes and adornment to maintain their sense of femininity and womanhood. But this desire to maintain femininity through clothes and adornment was a double-edged sword, and led to the assertion that black women could be easily bought with cheap trinkets.
18. This is incorrect: in 1970 *Life* put Sims on their cover under the caption "Breakthrough of Black Beauty". *Life*, February 1970.
19. Luna died in 1975 from a drugs overdose, and within her modeling career, Keenan argues that Luna was never able to break free of this stereotypical image of the exotic primitive (Keenan 1977: 176); this is also reflected in her late film career, notably in Federico Fellini's film *Satyricon*, where she plays a sex sorceress.
20. This image of black femininity in relationship to the Supremes is discussed in Nelson (1986: 88).

References

Books

Bogle, Donald. 1980. *Brown Sugar: Eighty Years of America's Black Female Superstars*. New York: Da Capo Paperbacks.
Bush, Barbara. 1981. "White Ladies, Coloured Favourites and Black Wenches." *Slavery and Abolition*, Vol. 2, No. 3 (December).
Carby, Hazel V. 1987. *Reconstructing Womanhood: The Emergence of the Afro-American Woman Novelist*. Oxford and New York: Oxford University Press.

Clifford, James. 1988. "Histories of the Tribal and the Modern." In idem, *Predicament of Culture*. Cambridge, MA and London: Harvard University Press.

Dabydeen, David. 1987. *Hogarth's Blacks: Images of Blacks in Eighteenth Century English Art*. Manchester: Manchester University Press.

Daniels, Walter. 1982. *Black Journals In The US: A Historical Guide To The World's Periodicals and Newspapers*. London: Greenwood Press.

Du Bois, W. B. 1982 [1902]. *Souls Of Black Folks*. Signet Classic. New York: New American Library.

Dyer, Richard. 1982. *Heavenly Bodies: Film Stars and Society*. London: BFI/Macmillan Education.

——. 1992 . "Four Films of Lana Turner." In idem, *Only Entertainment*. London and New York: Routledge.

Franklin Fraser, E. 1965. *Black Bourgeoisie: The Rise of A New Middle Class*. Free Press Paperback. London: Collier Macmillan.

Hall, Stuart. 1978. *Racism and Reaction: Five Views Of Multiracial Britain*. London: CRE.

Honor, Hugh. 1989. "The Image Of The Black In Western Art" No. 4, Part 2. Cambridge, MA and London: Harvard University Press.

hooks, bell. 1986. *Ain't I A Woman: Black Women and Feminism*. London: Pluto Press.

Keenan, Brigid. 1977. *The Women We Wanted To Look Like*. London: Macmillan.

Kuhn, A. 1986. *The Power Of The Image: Essays On Representation*. London and New York: Routledge.

Nelson, George. 1986. *Where Did Our Love Go*. London: Omnibus Press.

Rogoff, Irit. 2000. *Terra Infirma: Geography's Visual Culture*. London and New York: Routledge.

Sims, Naomi. 1979. *How To Be A Top Model*. Garden City, NY: Doubleday and Co., Inc.

Weigman, Robyn. 1991. "Black Bodies/American Commodities: Gender, Race and the Bourgeois Ideal in Contemporary Film." In *Unspeakable Images: Ethnicity and American Cinema*, ed. Lester D. Friedman. Urbana, IL: University of Illinois Press.

Newspapers and Magazines

Specific Authors

Applebaum, Sarah. 1964. "More On Desegregating Advertising." *Crisis*, February.

Summers, Barbara. 1987. "Model Firsts." *Essence*.

Toure, Halima. 1971. "The People Who Discovered the Beauty of Black." *Redbook*, March.

Wilson, Elizabeth. 1992. "Fashion and the Meaning of Life." *Guardian*, 18 May.

Young, A. S. ["Doc"]. 1963. "Beauty in Negro Women." *Sepia*, September.

Editorials and Features

"Can the Negro Model Make the Big Time?" 1954. *Ebony*, September.

"Dark Glamor." 1962. *Newsweek*, 3 September.

"Do Negro Women Overdress?" 1954. *Jet*, June.

Harper's Bazaar. 1965. April.

"Inventing The Black Consumer." 1992. *Ebony*, November.

Newsweek. 1963. 9 September.

Fashion Theory, Volume 6, Issue 1, pp. 83–110
Reprints available directly from the Publishers.
Photocopying permitted by licence only.

Bloody Jumpers: Benetton and the Mechanics of Cultural Exclusion

Paul Antick

Paul Antick is a photographer
and lecturer in Visual Culture
and Media at Middlesex
University, UK.

Each society has its regime of truth, its "general politics" of truth: that is, the types of discourses which it accepts and makes function as true; the mechanisms and instances which enable one to distinguish true and false statements, the means by which each value is sanctioned . . .

Michel Foucault in Rabinow 1984: 73.

Introduction

While the field of visual culture studies may occasionally consider advertising photography a useful historical indicator of a particular culture's "structure of feeling," (Williams 1965: 64) the position of relative inferiority it is held to occupy within the field of culture generally tends to preclude its inviting the same methods of critical enquiry that are often afforded to a wide variety of other media cultures. More specifically, in the relatively compact field of photography theory, advertising photography is generally considered to be beyond the bounds of any form of inquiry that seeks to understand (and produce) the photograph as a complex, multi-faceted and unpredictable object.

In other words, the establishing of advertising's identity within visual culture studies generally, and photography theory in particular, as *the* quintessential purveyor of dominant ideology in capitalist culture (particularly in relation to constructions of gender); its propensity to structure a "false" set of needs and desires; and its concomitant facilitation of a sense of "misrecognition" on the part of the viewing subject, have, arguably, constituted the theoretical boundaries within which most academic debates about advertising and photography have been allowed to take place.[1] In this way it could be argued that, instead of expanding and challenging the ways in which advertising photography is considered, reflected upon and analyzed in contemporary visual culture, photographic theory has actually succeeded in limiting the consideration of forms of encounter between advertising photography, consumers and cultural producers. By privileging one set of ideas about advertising photography above all others, photographic theory may have foreclosed the possibility of considering the ways in which advertisements do not simply establish and reproduce dominant cultural agendas but intersect with a multiplicity of other competing agendas and discourses articulated in, and in relation to, advertising itself.[2]

In the introduction to a recent collection of essays from the highly influential British photography magazine, *Camerawork*, Jessica Evans (1997) highlights the "need" for audience-based research in the field, and in so doing identifies one of the ways in which different possibilities for the analysis of photography might be explored within the field.

> It is to be hoped that the work developed in media studies by David Morley, Janice Radway and others on the ethnography of audiences, and that of Bourdieu on the habitus of audiences will be taken up in future work on photography, for we urgently need to incorporate a sense of the capacity for human agency into our analyses of photography and its uses (1997: 32).

What I would like to consider here is how this kind of work might happen in relation to that sphere of photographic production which is, arguably, negotiated by more people on a daily basis than any other but, at the same time, most denigrated within the field: advertising photography. The problem of how people make use of, and produce meanings in relation to, advertising photography is one that can be approached in several ways.

The approach I wish to focus on here, however, involves an examination of the relationship between advertising and its "significant others"—specifically, how making explicit the connections between advertising and its "others" can alert us to the ways in which the denigration of advertising might actually represent one of the ways in which, to paraphrase Stallybrass and White (1986), the high defines the low precisely in order to define itself as high, and, as such, the extent to which certain methodological orthodoxies—far from providing us with a set of impartial analytical tools—all too often collude in the reproduction of a set of socially anachronistic cultural taxonomies.

Suffice it to say that the theoretical perspectives alluded to above, indicative of most post-1970s photography theory, have largely emanated from academia. In the broader cultural context, however, there also exist a set of anxieties about advertising: anxieties that specifically informed the Benetton debate. These anxieties appear to be less bound up with the ideological nature of advertising photography, and more concerned with the ways in which certain advertising strategies, Benetton's in particular, might undermine a set of historically established discursive procedures that define, regulate and differentiate fields of culture—specifically, the ways in which different forms of knowledge are conventionally classified as either authentic or inauthentic; the cultural value ascribed different systems of representation; and the division of ethical labor among various institutions of culture.

In examining these concerns, I want to focus on Benetton's transgressions of certain visual or representational boundaries and consider the extent to which such transgressions may have both signaled and stimulated a profound re-alignment and re-evaluation of the role and status of informational culture (photography) in contemporary capitalist societies. In doing so I shall argue that the nature of the criticisms leveled against Benetton during the 1980s and early 1990s was indicative not only of the kinds of tensions that exist between different cultural institutions—advertising and the press, for instance—who suddenly find themselves in competition over the same cultural territory, but also of the tensions and contradictions that exist within specific institutions. Namely, advertising, the press and, to a lesser extent, academia.

In contemporary cultural theory it has become commonplace to suggest that the boundaries between different representational genres and cultural institutions, are becoming increasingly blurred.[3] Indeed, one could hold up Benetton's 1992 *Shock of Reality* campaign as an excellent example of this.[4] What is not conventionally acknowledged, however, is the extent to which the blurring of aesthetic boundaries can destabilize cultural institutions. An example of this is the kind of identity crisis sparked in the British press in relation to the *Shock of Reality* campaign. One symptom of this crisis might be the repeated implication in the press[5] that knowledge—articulated through documentary photography—considered instrumental in one context can be socially useful when deployed in another.

In order to unravel and evaluate the cultural and discursive implications of the criticisms leveled against *Shock of Reality* during the early 1990s, I intend to examine the ways in which Benetton's advertising campaigns, from *United Colors of Benetton* (1983) to *Shock of Reality* (1992), were themselves represented in a variety of journalistic and academic contexts. In doing so, I will concentrate on the ways in which certain statements were permitted to be made about Benetton at the expense of certain others; the extent to which these statements articulated a set of anxieties relating to the increasing difficulty that contemporary print media arguably have in reproducing certain key journalistic ideologies; and, finally, the ways in which the establishment of a particular set of "truths" about Benetton tended to preclude any critical consideration of the ways in which Benetton's adverts might actually have "worked" in specific historical and spatial contexts.

This article is not intended to act as a simplistic defence of advertising or advertising photography as such. Rather, I wish to draw attention to the ways in which the denigration and classification of advertising photography as a fundamentally "inauthentic" type of "speech act" can often serve to obfuscate the particularities of its communicative potential, specifically in relation to the ways in which particular adverts might use photography both to reinforce *and* subvert dominant ideologies in specific interpretative contexts.

Benetton, 1983–1991

According to Oliviero Toscani, Benetton's art director, photographer and, according to one *Arena* journalist, all-round "creative genius":[6] "Until 1983 . . . the nature of Benetton's advertising was clearly product oriented, showing the product and nothing else."[7] Toscani went on to suggest that Benetton's post-1983 campaigns represented a shift away from the "superficial" and "stupid" preoccupations of conventional advertising to what he called "issues of global concern."[8]

Toscani's reinvention of Benetton through these campaigns was significant for two reasons. First, in terms of the changes to the actual content of Benetton's adverts, and, secondly, because in being seen to refer to "social issues," Toscani—knowingly or not—was bidding to incorporate a set of values or knowledges, commonly associated with other more "legitimate" cultural institutions, into the lexicon of advertising. It could be said that the primary reason for this was to enhance Benetton's own cultural status in relation to, for example, the institutions of art and journalism.[9]

Thus, Toscani's first campaign, *All the Colors of The World*,[10] was intended to provide people with "food for *thought* with its images of happy . . . racially different children all laughing and smiling together" (Benetton Group 1993: 9). His subsequent campaign, *United World of*

Figure 1
United Colors of Benetton.
© Oliviero Toscani

Benetton ("a call for peace in the world" (Benetton Group 1993: 9) was followed by *United Colors of Benetton*, where, according to Toscani, ". . . [in] choosing models with accentuated ethnic features and names written in their own languages, the campaign strives for and achieves an image which is even more multi-racial and international" (1993: 9; Figure 1). This theme, in which racial, ethnic and cultural distinctions are both blurred by and redefined by Benetton—representing what Les Back and Vibeke Quaade, writing in *Third Text*, refer to as a "fantasy of multi-racial and inter-communal harmony" (1993: 65)—continued in the two subsequent campaigns: *United Fashions of Benetton* (1987) and *United Superstars* (1988).

However, although the thematic encoding of *United Colors* may have signaled a break with mass advertising's conventional thematic preoccupations, on a formal level *United Colors* still retained certain key generic features that not only enabled it to be firmly situated within the advertising genre—something facilitated by its use of young, conventionally good-looking models; high key lighting codes; the ubiquitous white studio backdrop; large-format camera technologies; and fine-grain film stock—but also prevented its being confused with representational forms characteristic of other, more legitimate, cultural institutions—journalism, for example—thus limiting the extent to which *their* epistemological and cultural legitimacy would have been threatened by the, admittedly limited, extent of Benetton's thematic transgressions during the 1980s.

However, despite the fact that between 1989 and 1991 Benetton's advertisements continued to "explore the subject of equality between blacks and whites" (Back and Quaade 1993: 11)—their rhetorical potency generated by what Back and Quaade refer to as "the stark presentation of racial oppositions" (1993: 68)—they also represented a far more radical

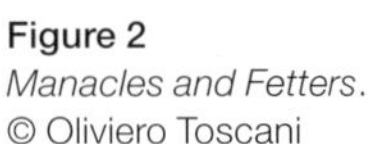

Figure 2
Manacles and Fetters.
© Oliviero Toscani

disruption of conventional advertising codes and techniques than had been achieved during the mid-1980s, something that was compounded by the absence of any iconographical reference to Benetton's "actual product."

In *Manacles and Fetters* (Figure 2),[11] for example, the conventionally "good-looking" models of previous campaigns have been replaced by a pair of anonymous lower torsos (one black, one white), clad in regulation-issue blue American prison uniforms, and joined together at the wrists by a pair of handcuffs. Arguably, it is the absence of certain key generic indicators—the fabulous face and body of the stereotypical fashion model—in this advertising image, as well as the way in which the photograph formally articulates concerns more often associated with "socially concerned" forms of photography (documentary, for example), that marked a defining moment in Benetton's gradual symbolic shift from advertiser to "social commentator"—a shift that was rendered conveniently confusing by their use of signifiers redolent of more "staged" (which is to say, "inauthentic") forms of photography, as well as a mode of representation that explicitly referred to certain postmodernist sub-genres of art photography. Perhaps the most obvious references to postmodernist art photography are to Andreas Serrano's stylized studio shots of "down and outs,"[12] which implicitly reference the documentary genre, but, in doing so, redefine, expand and apparently deconstruct it through an intertextually oblique selection and combination of generically disparate signifiers. Specifically, the viewer is potentially disarmed by Serrano's conflation of two mutually exclusive systems of representation, where dissolute figures from the American "underclass" are "lovingly" photographed against a plush, but muted, gray studio backdrop.

In the light of these formal and thematic shifts it was (perhaps predictably) significant that Benetton's tactics failed to present much of a threat to the ideological legitimacy of the art world, perhaps because Benetton's use of irony—commercially "interested" knitwear company playfully masquerading as socially concerned commentator—was something that could only ever enhance its position in relation to, and eventually even in, the postmodern art market—something that perhaps accounted for the success of Benetton's *Genitalia* at the 1993 Venice Biennale.[13]

However, despite the postmodern art world's unabashed enthusiasm for Benetton's advertising techniques, David A. Bailey (1989: 68) argued that "Benetton's campaign strateg[ies] foster the process . . . of 'object-ification,' in which cultural difference is commodified." For Bailey Benetton's postmodern playfulness, its transgression of representational boundaries, was reprehensible because, as Bailey remarked, "Benetton has commodified cultural difference as a marketing ploy." In other words ". . . the exploitation of particular stereotypical images of nations around the world serves the interest of Benetton as a seductive marketing device to sell and distribute their clothes worldwide" (1989: 64–5). Admittedly, it would be difficult to disagree with the oxymoronic point that Benetton's advertising strategies remained inextricably linked to a set of explicitly commercial business interests. But the idea that this in itself might be enough to invalidate, or worse, render unmentionable, those messages encoded in Benetton's advertisements is one that is worth taking up.

Bailey's suggestion that the reproduction of knowledge in a commercial context necessarily renders such knowledge "inauthentic" implicitly draws on the idea that there exist areas, or institutions, of knowledge that are "untainted" by the pollution of commerce. While I am not suggesting that knowledge is always a commodity, it is perhaps worth wondering why Bailey isolates the Benetton images for censure while failing to level the same criticism at the art world,[14] the print media or academia.

When, for instance, an "eye-catching" photograph of the destruction of the World Trade Center's Twin Towers appears on the front page of *The Guardian*,[15] one might argue that, as much as this image is part of a carefully orchestrated "consciousness-raising" strategy on the part of *The Guardian*, it is also involved in the everyday business of selling newspapers and, more to the point, satisfying the demands of those who choose to advertise on its pages. As Donna Schwartz points out (Brennen and Hardt 1999: 171), a newspaper's front page "can be conceived as an advertisement that sells the advertising inside the newspaper," and one of the ways in which this is achieved is precisely through the visual "pull" exerted by the drama played out in the documentary photograph.

Thus, given that even the most apparently disinterested forms of know-ledge—"quality" photojournalism, for example—are arguably always caught up with—and to some extent defined by—the vicissitudes of what Andrew Wernick calls "promotional culture,"[16] Bailey's objection to the objectification and commodification of race in Benetton's advertising campaigns begins to look problematic.

The Shock of Reality, 1992

It was as if the reality of suffering only had dignity and moral value in the editorial section of a newspaper and lost all its ability to denounce, and sensitise people when in contagious contact with advertising.

(Benetton Group 1993: 25).

In *Shock of Reality,* arguably Benetton's most contentious campaign to date, Benetton appropriated a variety of documentary photographs: *Family in Ohio, Boat People, Car Bomb, Flood, Murder, Refugees* and *Soldier* (Figures 3–6). These images were, according to Toscani, chosen because they apparently "express powerful human themes of global concern" (Benetton Group 1993: 12); the most notorious of which was *Family in Ohio*, an image that apparently depicted a man actually dying of Aids. Complaints about *Family in Ohio* (an image that only ever appeared in *The Face* (Jan. 1992)—that is, in the way it was originally intended to appear) were subsequently upheld by the British Advertising Standards Authority, who "deplored the advertiser's apparent willingness to provoke distress with their advertising approach" (*The Sunday Times* 26.1.1992). The "Aids ad" was subsequently condemned by advertising authorities in Italy, Holland, Spain, France and Belgium, as were four other images from the campaign.[17] "Nothing," Benetton modestly

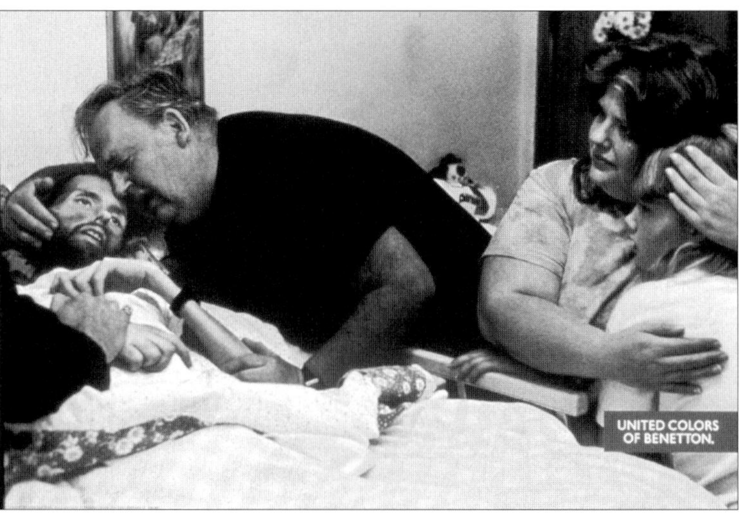

Figure 3
Family in Ohio.
© Oliviero Toscani

Figure 4
Refugees. © Oliviero Toscani

Figure 5
Boat People.
© Oliviero Toscani

Figure 6
Soldier. © Oliviero Toscani

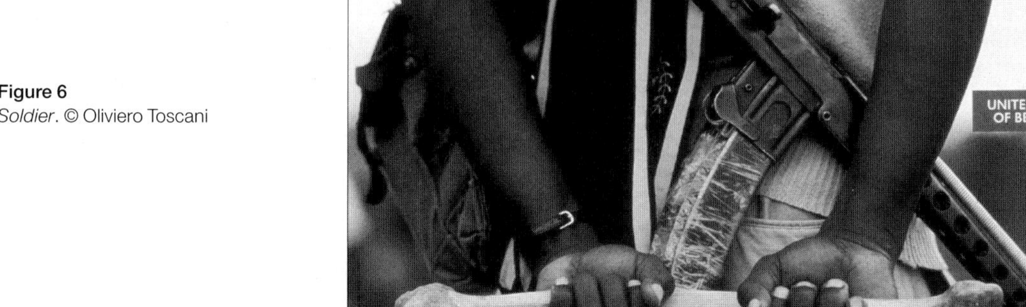

suggested, ". . . has shaken world opinion in relation to advertising as much as this campaign" (1993: 22).

Putting the issue of "world opinion" to one side, it is worth noting that, as well as generating sustained press hostility, *Shock of Reality* marked the wholesale appropriation by an advertiser of a completely "other" language (documentary photography) as well as the absolute dissolution of conventional advertising codes (apart from the ubiquitous brand logo).[18] Thus, *Shock of Reality* arguably represented a crucial symbolic break with the so-called "lies" and "superficiality" of advertising (something Benetton had never quite managed in its previous campaigns), as well as marking a kind of aesthetic and intertextual watershed for the advertising industry in general. A crucial symbolic threshold appeared to have been crossed with this campaign: the divide that separated "authentic" and "inauthentic" photographic aesthetics; and, arguably, it was precisely this that made *Shock of Reality* so intolerable for so many.

Commenting on *Family in Ohio*, *The Times* quotes a "spokesman" from the Advertising Standards Authority, ". . . we urge publishers to exercise their discretion so they do not carry an advert that would offend people . . . If this advert appears it is likely to be a depiction we would expect to get complaints about" (24.1.1992). Furthermore, according to Maggie Alderson, editor of *Elle*, "The advertising space for *Family in Ohio* was booked by Benetton well in advance for our next issue, but the copy arrived very late, and when we saw it we simply said: 'No way.'" (24.1.1992). Significantly, Alderson went on to say: "I remember seeing the photograph when it was in *Life* and thinking it was superb as a piece of photojournalism. But it has nothing to do with fashion and it has no place in a fashion magazine" (*Daily Mirror* 24.1.1992).

But what exactly was it that the Advertising Standards Authority, *The Times* and *Elle* found so objectionable about *Family in Ohio*? To answer this question—that is, in a way that goes beyond the "only doing it to sell jumpers" argument—we need to interrogate not just the form or content of the advertising image itself, but the discursive value that such images (and the institutions they "belong" to) are conventionally afforded in contemporary culture. Thus, if we acknowledge that Benetton's manufacturing of a novel kind of commodity aesthetic in *Shock of Reality* provided the press with an initial point of entry into the debate about the meaning of *Shock of Reality*, then perhaps it is worth going on to consider the extent to which press debate was, in part, sustained by a largely unconscious objection to the transgressive fusion of fashion and "hard news": a fusion that was made more difficult by the pollution of the masculine logic of documentary photojournalism with the "feminized" "pseudo-logic" of advertising, fashion advertising in particular. In other words, it was not only the alliance forged between documentary photography and the commodity form *per se* that stimulated negative press reactions, but the nature of the particular type of commodity with which the documentary photograph was associated.[19]

Just as the institution of fashion is bound up with notions of the ephemeral, fashion's identity—as well as its construction of identity—has conventionally been denigrated as "transient," "superficial" and "depthless"; values that not only characterize the subject of fashion and the institution of fashion as a whole, but that also stand in opposition to those pan-historical and transcendent values and qualities conventionally associated not only with "serious" journalism but also with the High Modernist art object as it is represented in traditional art histories and criticism.[20]

On the one hand, then, it was the drawing together of two symbolically disparate sign systems in *Family in Ohio* that was held to be so offensive: the conflation of the "real" world of documentary photography and the "superficial" world of middlebrow fashion advertising. On the other hand, however, it is also worth noting that what was considered equally reprehensible about this campaign was the juxtaposition of fashion—with its connotations of "brand newness"—with "death" and "degeneration", ideas conventionally associated with HIV/Aids.[21]

Thus, although Benetton's previous campaigns (from 1984 onwards) had attracted criticism, it had tended to concentrate on, for example, their multi-racial *content* and its mobilization for explicitly commercial purposes rather than the *form* that the advertising campaigns assumed. The press debate surrounding *Shock of Reality*, however, was largely fueled by an unconscious objection to Benetton's transgression and blurring of the symbolic and discursive boundaries that conventionally differentiate "hard news" from advertising generally, and to Benetton's "dumbing down" of the documentary photograph in particular.

Documentary Photography, Ideology and The Press

What is it then about documentary photography—and the type of knowledge it represents—that remains so precious that any perceived disturbance of its aesthetic and contextual integrity can provoke such emotive displays of collective hostility?

According to Howard Chapnick, former President of the Black Star Photo Agency, the "essence" of the photojournalistic image can be conceived of in terms of its depiction of a series of "implausible" and "inconceivable" events.[22] In other words, its particularity and specificity partly result from the distance it establishes between itself and the multitude of other photographic images that, arguably, represent what they themselves constitute: that is, the banality of the image world in everyday life. The advertising image would represent perhaps—from a photojournalistic point of view—a prime example of this.

Furthermore, according to Michael Griffen, the legitimacy of the photojournalistic image is ultimately realized through its production of *affect*. In other words, as a result of the photographer's production of "high drama and emotional pull"—the conventional aesthetic criteria by which most successful documentary photographs are judged—it is held that an effective documentary photograph will be capable of transforming the mood of the viewer—which is to say that he or she will be "moved" by it.[23]

One might argue, however, that the realization of affect relies as much on the relationship between the documentary photograph and the "ideology of realism"[24]—which frames the discursive conditions of its production and consumption—as it does on anything in the image itself. Consequently, the production of affect, rather than being contingent on the form that any one image assumes, is actually an effect of the viewer's belief in the *veracity* of the documentary image (something that is certainly encouraged but not wholly determined by its form); and it is this that enables one to be "moved" by it in a way one would not necessarily be moved by an advertising image, however "moving" *its* content might appear to be.

It is worth noting that although documentary photography has been subject to the deconstructive ire of photography theory since the mid-1970s, as well as a variety of aesthetic changes since its inception as a mass media form,[25] its basic ideological function (its facility to render the world "as it is"; to provide an "eyewitness" account of what Roland Barthes refers to as *"that* [which]—*has—been"* (Barthes 1982: 82)—a function that exists in contradistinction to the function of the "artificial" world of fashion photography), has remained intact. In other words, the documentary photograph has continued to maintain its ideological grip on the social imaginary, in spite of the academic broadsides leveled against it and the various ways in which the form of the documentary photograph has evolved historically.[26] So, while various technical and critical interventions may have modified the actual form of the documentary photograph, as well as its reception in certain restricted contexts, they have not impacted on its popular epistemological status.

How then, in this context, has the commodity aspect of documentary photography been disavowed in such a way as to secure its position as a privileged form of objective knowledge? *To what ends* is the myth of documentary photography's disinterestedness sustained by those institutions for which it performs such a vital role?[27] In a journalistic context the photograph's promotional role is repressed by a set of historically established discursive procedures,[28] which constrain the ways in which the documentary photograph is received by its audience.[29] In relation to *Shock of Reality*, the invalidation of advertising, coupled with a reiteration of the "integrity" of the documentary project, as it exists within a journalistic context, clearly provided the discursive framework through which most press criticism was refracted.

Arguably, however, the press's attack on Benetton, and its parallel defence of documentary photography, betrayed another set of concerns, arguably linked to the fragility of the press's self-image. In other words, the press's assault on Benetton might not only represent a specific crisis of institutional identity, primarily made manifest through Benetton's use and abuse of an assortment of documentary photographs, but a reaction that may be seen as nothing less than a symptom of a more deep-seated *malaise*. In other words, what was ultimately significant was not just Benetton's instrumental use of documentary photography, but also the way in which Benetton effectively obliged the press to unconsciously re-evaluate its own status as a commercially disinterested institution.

The Press's Repressed

The business of journalism seems to be impinging on the basic functions of journalism in a way that is ultimately dangerous to journalism and perilous to the public interest. Across a broad spectrum of news organizations, the balance between the bottom line and professional news judgements, between journalism's private and public functions, has been tilting toward the forces of the market place and maximum return and away from the newsrooms—and the public interest.

> Former *Washington Post* correspondent Dan Oberdorfer,
> quoted in Sparrow (1999: 3)

Like the documentary photograph, the press is conventionally held to be a privileged eyewitness to world events. Moreover, its primary role in "civilized" liberal society is, again like the documentary photograph, to relay such events to the general public in a reasonable and disinterested fashion (see Schwartz in Brennen and Hardt 1999). In being seen (or at least imagined) to be doing this, the press has come to represent what Thomas Carlyle described as a "Fourth Estate" (Powe 1991: 261)—in other words, "a political institution able to act independently . . . and, therefore one capable of safeguarding democracy" (Sparrow 1999: 3). Given its position of privilege in relation to other institutions of culture (a privilege secured in the US, where the press—unlike any other American industry—is protected under the American constitution's "right to free speech") it is not difficult to understand why the bringing into question of press impartiality should elicit such a defensive response from the industry.

Jacques Lacan's remarks about the formation and comprehension of identity may be useful here.[30] Although Lacan is referring to the ways in which individual subjectivities are constituted, it is possible to understand his argument in relation to the ways in which an *institution* might potentially misrecognize itself. Indeed, it appears to be precisely the way in which the "I" of the press misrecognizes itself[31] in the mirror of journalistic ideology, effectively repressing the material conditions that constitute its identity, that serves to perpetuate the "un-real" image the press continues to have of itself.

That the psychic history of the press can be characterized by the fraught relationship that exists between its commercial aspect on the one hand and, on the other, its status as disseminator *par excellence* of value-free knowledge means that, given the immiscible relationship that exists between these two aspects of the press, it is hardly surprising that for its "disinterested" side to maintain a position of ideological pre-eminence in relation to its "other," its "other" must be evacuated in order to avoid any unnecessary epistemological and discursive complications.

Thus it is precisely that sense of incoherence and fragmentation—the coexistence of contradictory properties in the same body—that, for Lacan, is fundamentally constitutive of identity that is not only refused by the press (for good ideological reasons, perhaps) but that is "returned" to it in the cracked mirror of *Shock of Reality*—as a result, that is, of Benetton's redeploying the documentary photograph in an unambiguously commercial context. Indeed, it was precisely the conflation of the worlds of documentary photojournalism and business commerce in *Shock of Reality* that served to draw attention to the contradictions that remain largely unacknowledged in the press itself—that perhaps rendered *Shock of Reality* so uncannily disarming.

Moreover, one might argue that the more press organizations become indistinguishable from the variety of other related business concerns with which they are increasingly being linked, the greater the likelihood that the integrity of the press will be even more difficult to maintain. Consequently, the return of the press's repressed, as it has been returned in an age of global mass media monopolization involving the integration of the entertainment and information industries, for example, represents perhaps a partial—and heavily disguised—acknowledgment on the part of the press itself that it is actually not so very far removed from the thing it strives to define itself against.[32]

Indeed, in the light of this one could just as easily ask the question: precisely how ethical is it for the press to use Aids to sell newspapers ? It would, I think, be ridiculous to suggest that, because the press is as subject to the diktats and whims of the market-place as a fashion company is, anything one might find in the press is necessarily rendered invalid. By the same token, however, I would argue that this is also potentially true of fashion photography and advertising.

Relocating "Family in Ohio"

Having outlined the ways in which a set of discursive procedures—largely organized around issues of commodification, gender, race, photography and advertising—were deployed in relation to Benetton's advertising campaigns during the 1980s and early 1990s effectively to prohibit consideration of their impact on the social imaginary, I now want to imagine what might have been. In other words, I want to offer some informed speculations regarding the ways in which *Family in Ohio* not only intersected with a variety of other Aids-related "utterances" in Britain, but positively contributed, in a moderately subversive fashion, to oppositional Aids-related discourses elsewhere.

As I have implied, issues of context and interpretation in relation to *Shock of Reality* are conveniently elided by Bailey et al. by virtue of the ways in which they fetishize the sphere of production, to the extent that any consideration of the ways in which the discursive environments within which *Shock of Reality* was actually situated may have shaped the variety of ways in which it was consumed becomes pointless.

Having said that, even where meaning is considered as something other than a straightforward effect of the image's commodity status, this is generally done in such a way as to prevent any critical evaluation of the relationships between a particular advertising photograph, its exhibition in a specific cultural context and, finally, its reception. Arguably, this mode of analysis does the important ideological work of naturalizing or rendering commonsensical the relationship between a "tainted" sphere of image production (mass advertising) and the inevitability of its "react-ionary" messages; an outcome of what White, writing in *The Sunday Times* (1992), refers to as the unacceptable "imbroglio of sweaters and morals."[33]

This isn't to say that the content of *Shock of Reality* may not amount to the reproduction and dissemination of a series of "reactionary" messages in relation to HIV/Aids. However, in order to assess this, it is worth considering the ways in which specific advertising images have been deployed in a variety of historically specific and discursively uneven contexts. As one such example, I want to consider the ways in which Benetton's most notorious *Shock of Reality* ad intersected with a variety of Aids-related utterances in Britain and Italy. In doing this I want to consider how those utterances could be understood as having inflected *Family in Ohio* with strikingly different sets of meanings and significances.

To begin with, it is worth noting that *Family in Ohio* evokes an atmosphere of religiosity. This is suggested by the depiction of a bed-ridden Christ-like figure; a painting directly above his head featuring the image of a man with outstretched arms, dressed in Christ-like robes; and a black-clad arm (suggestive of a priest) entering the image from left of frame, uncannily echoing the outstretched arms featured in the painting. Furthermore, although *Family in Ohio* certainly appears to make explicit reference to documentary photography (a reference reinforced by the swathes of comment surrounding it) it also refers to a variety of other sign systems. Indeed, Oliviero Toscani refers to this image as a "modern-day *pieta*" (1993: 36); that is, "a representation of the dead Christ . . . in which the sufferings of Christ are exaggerated and distorted" (Murray 1978: 345).

On one level then, the kinds of religious connotations identified above might constitute a "positive" message about HIV and Aids—one that, in Britain, may be understood as a reaction against the type of "negative" Aids imagery that came to characterize dominant media representations of the illness, particularly during the 1980s and early 1990s.[34] Thus, in contrast with those representations of Aids that suggest, as Simon Watney (1987) implies, that people with Aids have "brought it on themselves and, therefore, deserve everything they get," what we, arguably, have in *Family in Ohio* is an image that re-articulates Aids as a curiously privileged condition: synonymous with spiritual transcendence, resurrection and an intimacy with God.

Having suggested one of the ways in which *Family in Ohio* may be understood as a "positive" reaction to the kinds of negative Aids imagery Simon Watney refers to in *Ten 8*, we might, on the other hand, argue that, in fact, *Family in Ohio* actually represents an equally polarized point of view where individuals suffering with Aids are crassly figured as quasi-religious figures whose physical martyrdom through Aids ludicrously signifies a first, feeble step on the rocky road to spiritual redemption. As Roger Clarke, writing in *The Guardian* about popular, liberal represent-ations of Aids, remarks, "We make a saint of Derek Jarman, a fallen angel of Bruce Chatwin and a Madonna of the Princess of Wales" (1.12.1994). Thus, inasmuch as the physical suffering of Aids becomes synonymous with "spiritual health" (ibid.) *Family in Ohio* may arguably be seen to contain another "negative" message, inasmuch as Aids here is hysterically romanticized by Benetton—to such an extent that the actual ways in which most ordinary mortals experience dying from an Aids-related illness—(a frightening "shitty" thing where "nothing is resolved")—remain unspoken. It is perhaps an example of cruel irony that Benetton chose to describe this image as showing us the "*reality* of suffering" (Benetton Group 1993: 25, my italics).

However, even if the kind of "alternative Aids myth" I have provisionally identified in Benetton's *Family in Ohio* actually operates to foment further the climate of cultural negativity that arguably exists in relation to Aids, any serious evaluation of the extent to which *Family in Ohio* represents a fundamentally reactionary mythologization of Aids must surely be measured against its relationship with all those other images of Aids in circulation in Britain at the time and immediately prior to it. In other words, it may be the case that, in an ideal world, the reactionary nature of *Family in Ohio* would go without saying; but in a world where messages or sign values are constantly in competition for positions of hegemonic pre-eminence one could argue that, however ideologically imperfect *Family in Ohio* might be, it does, at the very least, represent a flawed attempt to subvert and displace those images constitutive of an especially virulent type of Aids-related discourse—images largely situated in the field of popular journalism. Which is to say that *Family in Ohio*'s ideological or discursive significance is as much a consequence of the specificity of its relationship with a host of other images as it is an effect of its semiotic singularity.

However, in suggesting some of the potentially contradictory ways in which *Family in Ohio* may have operated in one particular social context, it is worth pointing out that this is not a guarantee that *Family in Ohio* would have performed a similar task elsewhere. Which is to say that, even if its apparently implicit idealization of Aids continued to inform its reception outside Britain, the cultural and political value afforded to such an idealization may have varied dramatically from context to context.

Bearing this in mind, I want to consider the social, ideological and political climate pertaining to Aids-related issues in Italy in 1992 and the cultural value that *Family in Ohio* was afforded in this particular context.

On 10 November 1992 *The Guardian* reported that ". . . a young middle-class Roman (A.G.) wrote at length about his solitude, his shame and his thoughts of suicide . . . to the editor of *La Stampa*, the Italian newspaper. *La Stampa* published his appeal in full on the front page and triggered a nationwide debate about AIDS, which has never been confronted head on in a country where unspoken but strict religious and social codes mean such issues are taboo." Following its appearance in *La Stampa*, *The Guardian* went on to report that the story of "A.G." ". . . was leading the national television news and becoming a topic in bars" (ibid.) Furthermore, *The Guardian* stated that "The controversy over an advertisement by clothing manufacturer Benetton featuring an AIDS death-bed . . . [had] kept the issue in the news" (ibid.).

I am not suggesting that *Family in Ohio* was single-handedly responsible for a sudden turnaround in dominant attitudes towards Aids in Italy at this time. But, clearly, investing "Aids sufferers" with Christ-like connotations in a country where the Catholic Church arguably represents the key player in terms of the definition and reproduction of the dominant moral and ethical codes, was a strategy that afforded *Family in Ohio* the kind of incendiary ideological status it could never have acquired in Britain. The fact that the Church in Italy had largely defined Aids using, to paraphrase Back and Quaade (1993), "the grammar of religion" (Aids being conventionally figured as a kind of "divine retribution" visited on various amoral types, i.e. homosexual "perverts" and drug addicts) meant that *Family in Ohio's* evocation of a type of alternative, and fundamentally redemptive, Aids myth, relying upon and ultimately subverting the "grammar of religion," would have afforded it considerable cultural weight. Moreover, given that Aids is generally represented in terms of its being a "gay disease," the conflation of Christ with the idea of a gay man would have had added significance.

The Guardian reports A.G. as saying, ". . . because of my homosexuality I have been close to suicide many times, but a sense of the power of life and Christ himself stopped me" (10.11.1992). Thus it is possible to understand *Family in Ohio*, as it existed in an Italian context, not as simply alerting the world to a set of "issues of global concern," as Toscani would have us believe, but as intersecting with a constellation of interwoven discourses where it was not just the meaning of Aids that was at stake, but the meaning of Christ and, by implication, the veracity of dominant forms of Christianity—in other words, the authority and legitimacy of the Roman Catholic Church itself.

Conclusion

Clearly, taking into account the social, political and discursive climates within which advertisements such as Benetton's inevitably find themselves situated brings into question the usefulness of methodologies that dwell exclusively on the commercially driven nature of the advertising industry. In many ways, however, it would be counter-productive to argue that because advertising photography may operate in ways that cannot simply be reduced to "the reproduction of dominant ideologies" or "the misrecognition of the self" it is, therefore, not ideological at all. The point is, perhaps, to acknowledge that while advertisements can sometimes perform several different, often contradictory, tasks at the same time, it is worth paying close attention not only to the specificities of any given advertising campaign but also the precise nature of those evaluative techniques or tools one brings to bear upon them. In doing so one should ideally become sensitive to the ways in which such tools can work to conceal as much as they reveal. Thus, as Victor Burgin saliently points out, "The question is not 'Is this tool better than that tool?' The question is rather 'What tool is best suited for this particular job?'" (Evans 1997: 75).

Acknowledgments

Thanks to Benetton for allowing me to reproduce their advertising images.

Notes

1. See Victor Burgin's "Looking at Photographs" and "Photography, Phantasy, Function" in Burgin (1982). Here Burgin echoes the theoretical sentiments expressed in "Screen Theory" when he states that "Photography is one signifying system among others in society which *produces* the ideological subject in the same movement in which they 'communicate' their ostensible 'contents'" (1982: 153). It is worth noting that Burgin's emphasis on the seemingly effortless production of the subject of ideology *in* photography is one that still characterizes much contemporary photography theory. For a more recent example of this approach see Hirsch (1997). The essay that, perhaps, best characterizes the theoretical position assumed by *Screen*—which, broadly speaking represented an amalgam of Lacanian psychoanalysis and Althusserian Marxism; what Mulvey refers to as "political psychoanalysis" (1975: 6)—is Laura Mulvey's "Visual Pleasure and Narrative Cinema" in *Screen* 16(3), Autumn 1975, p. 6. Here Mulvey evaluates the ways in which the visual conventions of popular cinema structure and prescribe the female subjects' identification with an alienated, and alienating, representation of femininity that is always, according to Mulvey, ". . . displayed for the gaze and enjoyment of men," whom she describes as the "the active controllers of the look . . ." (1975: 13). As Marianne Hirsch points out, "Mulvey is writing about the film camera and not about still images but . . . in its reception, her argument has been and can be extended to the camera gaze more generally" (1997). For an incisive critique of "Screen Theory" see Paul Willemen's "Notes on Subjectivity" in *Screen* 19(1) and Morley (1992: 59–71). Willemen (1978) suggests, in relation to "Screen Theory," that "There remains an unbridgeable gap between 'real' readers/authors and 'inscribed' ones. Constructed and marked in and by the text, real readers are subjects in history, living in social formations, rather than mere subjects of a single text. The two types of subject are not commensurate. But for the purposes of formalism, real readers are supposed to coincide with the constructed readers." Similarly, Morley suggests that ". . . psychoanalytically based work has ultimately mobilized what can be seen as another version of the hypodermic theory of effects (see Adorno and Horkheimer 1972)—in so far as it is, at least in its initial and fundamental formulations, a universalist theory which attempts to account for the way in which the subject is necessarily positioned by the text" (1992: 59). He goes on to state that: "The text . . . may offer the subject specific positions of intelligibility, it may operate to prefer certain readings above others; what

it cannot do is to guarantee them – that must always be an empirical question" (1992: 71).

2. See, for example, Berger 1972 (especially Ch. 7, which represents a condensed version of some of the arguments presented in Debord 1967); see also Williamson (1982); Victor Burgin's "Art, Common Sense and Photography" in Evans (1997) (and its theoretical precursor, Roland Barthes "The Rhetoric of the Image" in Barthes 1977); and Myers 1986.

3. Indicative, perhaps, of the extent to which such a cultural "common sense" now routinely informs debates in popular culture is the appearance in *Dazed and Confused* of Rachel Ames's "*Austrian Label, Wendy & Jim Blurring The Boundaries Between Fashion and Art*" (Ames 2001). For an example of the ways in which academic debate is beginning to question some of the epistemological and conceptual difficulties attendant on "the blurring of boundaries" see Coles and Defert (2000).

4. The advertising campaign *The Shock of Reality* of spring 1992 marked a new step in Benetton's campaign strategies: the seven images presented were not traditionally commissioned fashion images, but actual documentary photographs taken by photo journalists and already published in newspapers and magazines. The subjects, in accordance with the "corporate philosophy of information and concern" (http://www.benetton.com/wws/aboutyou/ucdo/reality/file1848.html), included: an obscure and insidious illness; violence and intimidation; forced emigration; natural catastrophes.

5. See also G. Adair, "In the name of God, go stick it up your jumpers" in *The Guardian* 13.2.1992; Anon, "Benetton profits from controversy" in *The Times* 28.3.1992; P. Corrias, "Beneath Jumpers" in *The Guardian* 8.6.1993; J. Erlichman, "Benetton defends shock tactics as art" in *The Guardian* 20.2.1992; A. Fresco, "Benetton uses Aids victim in advert" in *The Guardian* 24.1.1992; S. Moore, "Graphic Violence" in *The Guardian* 2.10.1993; J. Moir, "Ad Nauseum" in *The Guardian* 11.2.1995; J. Mullin, "Benetton plays new card in rolling back the frontiers of shock" in *The Guardian* 24.1.1992; N. North, "Sick! Benetton Use Dying Aids Man" in *The Daily Mirror* 25.1.1992; I. Webb, "One jumper ahead of the pack" in *The Times* 15.1.1994; C. White, "Blood, sweaters and designer tears" in *The Sunday Times* 16.2.1992.

6. Russell 1993: 25.

7. Benetton Group 1993: 9.

8. According to the writers of the official Benetton Web Site (http://www.benetton.com/wws/aboutyou/ucdo/race/file1847.html) Benetton started its "Campaigns for Racial Equality" when Oliviero Toscani's first photographs, in which different races are seen living in harmony, were used in the advertising campaigns of 1984. Benetton's new communication strategy began this campaign entitled "All the Colors of the World," which included "ads which spotlight groups of young

people of different races and colors as they play and laugh together. This campaign appeared in 14 countries and sparked off yet another racial polemic in South Africa: the photos featuring white and black youths together published in magazines targeted at the black population were refused by publications reserved for whites."

9. There are three ways in which this strategy was, and continues to be, realized. First, through Benetton's gradual, and discontinuous, appropriation of signs conventionally held to belong to a set of discursively opposing institutions—a strategy complemented by the dissolution of sign structures that constitute the visual and linguistic rhetoric of conventional advertising images generally, prior, that is, to the early-mid-1980s. Secondly, through a sustained mythologization of the "visionary idiosyncrasies" of Oliviero Toscani himself, Benetton's former "artist in residence"; and thirdly, through the investment in Benetton of "oppositional" values, something which is largely realized through the circulation of Benetton's own secondary promotional materials (*Colors* magazine, press releases, catalogs etc.) as well as the various ways in which Benetton's campaign style was (and is) represented in both the press and academe—this article being yet another example. For an example of recent press coverage see Clark (2000).

10. http://www.benetton.com/wws/aboutyou/ucdo/race/file1847.html.

11. Toscani *Manacles and Fetters* (also known as "handcuffs"), Benetton Advertising campaign, 1989, see *http://www.benetton.com/wws/ aboutyou/ucdo/race/file1846.html*

12. See "Nomads" in Andreas Serrano, *Body and Soul*, Takarajima Books, 1995.

13. A selection of Benetton's advertising images were also featured in shows at the Musée D'Art Contemporain, Lausanne, Switzerland, *Benetton par Toscani* (1995); and the Museo de Arte Moderno, Mexico City, Mexico, *Toscani Al Muro: 10 anos de imagenes para United Colors of Benetton* (Mantle 1999: 314).

14. See the section on dealerships in Nairne (1987).

15. Spencer Platt, *The Guardian*, 12 September 2001.

16. According to Wernick, ". . . with the development of the market, promotion is a condition which has increasingly befallen discourses of all kinds; and the more it has done so, the more its modalities and relations have come to shape the formation of culture as a whole," quoted in Lee 2000: 305.

17. Of the seven images produced for display on billboards and magazines in Europe, five were either subject to court injunctions or voluntary bans: *Soldier*, France; *Family in Ohio*, Britain and Spain; *Soldier*, Britain; *Car*, Ireland (Benetton Group 1993: 173).

18. In the light of this, it is interesting how many students in my own department at Middlesex University have remarked, when confronted with an especially powerful documentary image, that, although they

can't be exactly sure where it comes from, it is, in their opinion, just as likely to be a Benetton advert as anything else. Arguably then, branding a product with an immediately identifiable and distinctive set of visual signs—the color-saturated documentary photograph, for example—could easily obviate the need to reference the brand logo altogether. Thus, as much as Benetton's appropriation of documentary photography might have effected a re-branding of Benetton, it also potentially represented, for many people, the re-branding of documentary photography itself.

19. According to Stuart Ewen, during the early years of what Michell Aglietta refers to as the Fordist "regime of accumulation," "the primary function of advertising was the creation and stimulation of new consumer needs as well as to sell the system of mass consumption itself" (1976: 90). Thus, where "commodity consumption became the natural means to need satisfaction" advertising was the "critical intermediary agency bridging the industrial process and everyday life" (Ewen 1976: 93). Furthermore, in the visual rhetoric of advertising photography, men were largely featured as the producers of goods and women as the producers of domestic lifestyles, which were always—according to the logic of advertising discourse—contingent on the goods being made available to them by the men who labored away on the proverbial Fordist production line. The development of advertising, and advertising photography, then, became not only the "means by which women could be educated into the correct modes of consumption" (Ewen 1976: 95) but also the way in which women's sense of their own social identity came to be constituted in relation to the "soft," "cosmetic," "fantasy-oriented" world of advertising itself. Furthermore, in the same way that these values coalesced around the sign "woman," so the idea of the "feminine" arguably came to define the cultural and discursive value of advertising knowledge itself. Thus, not only did the process of consumption become feminized, but the institution of advertising and—by implication—the knowledge it furnished the world with acquired a "soft" or feminine gloss. In addition, I would suggest that fashion discourse, as it is articulated through fashion photography in advertising, constitutes the very apotheosis of "soft knowledge" in contemporary capitalist culture. First, because fashion—unlike "hard" news— is generally considered to be solely preoccupied with the body in particular and the commodity form in general, something that has historically facilitated its classification as "superficial" or, worse still, "trivial." So, where "serious" journalism does the work of fostering the reproduction of universal values (conventionally synthesizing a particular news event through a set of blanket, humanistic principles and beliefs intended to "unite the populace" (Schwartz in Brenen and Hardt 1999: 162)), fashion is held to cast its "unethical" and immaterial eye upon a collection of disparate bodily forms whose

social identities are constituted through a set of transient, and, therefore, culturally insignificant, desires and passions.

20. Particularly where the value of the art object—be it "modern" or "postmodern"—is constructed according to a set of evaluative techniques and procedures characteristic of High Modernist criticism, i.e. where the measure of a "good" piece of art is determined by the extent to which it is perceived to satisfy a set of criteria—organized around notions of authorial intent, aesthetic integrity etc.—that pre-exist the object itself.

21. *The Guardian* quotes "Aids expert" Nick Partridge, "acting chief executive of Aids charity, The Terrence Higgins Trust" thus: "Using the distressing depiction of any form of serious illness or deathbed scene to sell clothing for commercial profit is offensive. Benetton is trying to cash in on the plight of millions dying from Aids." Significantly, Partridge is also quoted as saying that ". . . not only is the ad. offensive, but it leaves me wondering what Benetton is trying to communicate to the general public" (24.1.1992).

22. Quoted in Michael Griffen, "The Great War Photographs: Constructing Myths of History and Photojournalism" in Brennen and Hardt 1999: 128.

23. Michael Griffen in Bremen and Hardt 1999: 129.

24. See Taylor 1998: 52–6. See also Martha Rosler, "In around, and afterthoughts (on documentary photography)" in Bolton 1992; Pierre Bourdieu *The Social Definition of Photography* in Evans and Hall (eds), 1999 and Abigail Solomon-Godeau 1991. According to Solomon-Godeau, "the documentary photograph . . . is 'spoken' within language and culture; its meanings are both produced and secured within those systems of representation that *a priori* mark its subject—and our relations to the subject—in preordained ways. The fact that a photograph appears to speak itself, as do realist forms in general, should alert us . . . to the working of ideology which always functions to naturalize the cultural" 1991: 171.

25. See Solomon-Godeau 1991: 171.

26. The historical evolution of the documentary photograph would include such things as its incorporation of color; its appropriation of surrealist aesthetics (see, for example, Humphrey Jennings's Mass Observation project and, more recently, the work of Magnum photographer, Martin Parr); and, most significantly perhaps, the ways in which it has embraced a variety of innovative photographic technologies; 35mm film, faster lenses, etc.

27. It is worth noting, in relation to criticisms of Benetton's use of documentary, that if a documentary photograph can only retain its "authenticity" within a particular institutional context—a point of view that underpins objections voiced in the press and, to a lesser extent, academe—then the idea that there is something inherently truthful about the documentary image itself is obviously brought into

question. It is ironic perhaps that we, as newspaper readers, are as much alerted to the contingent nature of photographic meaning by the ways in which the debate about Benetton was structured in the British press and print media—institutions for which the inherent veracity and truthfulness of the documentary photograph, are arguably, inestimable—as we are by anything in the images themselves. See also Donna Schwartz's remarks on "the establishment of photojournalism as an objective reportorial strategy" (in Brennen and Hardt 1999).

28. "The advertising is exploitative" wrote Helen Fielding in *The Times*, "because it is using Aids to sell jumpers" (26.1.1992); the implication being that if a story about Aids was being used to sell newspapers it would somehow be more acceptable. Fielding goes on to ask, "Where is the social commitment? What does the Benetton group sponsor with its wealth? Aids research? Help for the world's poor? No: Formula 1 racing, a basketball team and one or two small arts projects in Italy" (26.1.1992). Significantly, this is a demand that can only be made of Benetton—and not News International, for example—precisely because the press refused to allow Benetton's communicative pretensions a legitimate position within its own normalizing discourse—a discourse within which any ideological difficulties consumers might potentially have had, in relation to a particular cultural institution's moral responsibilities, were resolved through the construction of an arbitrary institutional division of ethical labor. In other words, consumers were invited by the press to identify Benetton as an "inauthentic," self-interested knitwear company and News International as a purveyor of "authentic," "objective" and "impartial" knowledge. Hence the inevitability of the numerous calls made in the press urging Benetton to donate money to Aids charities (24.1.1992)—something that, to my knowledge, no one ever demanded of News International, The Mirror Group or Tony O'Reilly, owner of *The Independent*.

29. Arguably, a similar set of constraints proscribe the ways in which academic texts are received. Here I would suggest that it is equally problematic to suggest that the production and circulation of "intellectual" knowledge remains free from the constraints of the market. The commercial nature of relationships between academic publishing houses and intellectuals; the ways in which prestige and status afforded intellectuals by their publishing successes are often translated into forms of financial remuneration by their employers; the commodified nature of higher education, inasmuch as students, nowadays, are construed as much as "consumers" as they are "scholars"; and the relationship between the research assessment exercise in Britain, departmental funding and the concomitant proliferation of juried academic journals surely renders any claim for the autonomous nature of academic production extremely dubious. See Andrew

Wernick (in Lee 2000) for a discussion of the commodified nature of Higher Education and Bourdieu 1988 for a provocative account of the relationship between the production of academic knowledge and the instrumental position it occupies within the Academy.

30. See Jacques Lacan, "The Mirror Stage as Formative of the Function of the I as Revealed in Psychoanalytic Experience" in Lacan 1977.

31. For a concise and extremely clear account of Lacan's theory of the "Mirror Stage," where, according to Lacan, the subject is enjoined to identify with "a mirage of himself, outside of himself" 1975: 140) see Bowie 1991: 17–43.

32. One can appreciate the ways in which economic imperatives can explicitly determine news content by considering the extent and consequences of Rupert Murdoch's News International's aggressive drive towards vertical integration—that is, the acquisition of companies involved in the production of the same product. For example, as part of News International's shift from content provider to global distributor, Murdoch "purchased Hong Kong's Star TV satellite system in July 1993; Star also carried BBC World. However, because the Chinese authorities did not want the BBC's coverage entering China from Hong Kong, Murdoch dropped the BBC from Star" (Sparrow 1999: 100). For a useful account of the political and financial consequences of the interrelatedness of different media organizations owned by the same parent multinational, and their propensity for self-promotion (the *Sun* providing favorable coverage of BSKyB, for example) see Peter Golding and Graham Murdoch's discussion of "media synergy," "Culture, Communications and Political Economy" in Curran and Gurevitch 2000: 70–93.

33. This mode of analysis is exemplified by Back and Quaade, who argue in relation to *United Colors* that "images of human difference are fixed within Benetton's discourse" and that ". . . race and ethnicity are presented as essentially unchanging and eternal social categories" (1993: 68).

34. Watney states that "I am not aware of a single photojournalistic Aids narrative published in the United Kingdom which does not collude in every respect with the overall discursive tendency to criminalise and stigmatise its hapless subjects" (1987: 22). Also, for a concise discussion of media representations of Aids in the British press during the 1980s and 1990s, see Eldridge, Kitzinger and Williams 1997: 60–72.

References

Adorno, Theodor and Max Horkheimer. 1972. *The Dialectic of Enlightenment*. New York: Herder and Herder.

Ames, Rachel. 2001. "Austrian Label, Wendy & Jim Blurring The Boundaries Between Fashion and Art," *Dazed and Confused*, 76 (April).

Back, L. and V. Quaade. 1993. "Dream Utopias, Nightmare Realities: Imaging Race and Culture within the world of Benetton Ads". *Third Text* No. 22 (Spring).

Bailey, David A. 1989. "Product Branding the World", In Paul Wombell (ed.), *The Globe: Representing the World*. York: Impressions Gallery of Photography.

Barthes, Roland. 1977. *Image-Music-Text*. London: Fontana.

——. 1982. *Camera Lucida*. Glasgow: Jonathan Cape.

Benetton Group. 1993. *Global Vision—United Colors of Benetton*. Rabundo: Benetton Group.

Berger, John. 1972. *Ways of Seeing*. London: Penguin.

Bolton, Richard. (ed.). 1992. *The Contest of Meaning*, Cambridge, MA: MIT Press.

Bourdieu, Pierre. 1988. *Homo Academicus*. Cambridge: Polity Press.

Bowie, Malcolm. 1991. *Lacan*, London: Fontana Press.

Brennen, B. and H. Hardt. 1999. *Picturing the Past: Media, History and Photography*. Urbana, Il: University of Illinois Press.

Burgin, Victor. (ed.). 1982. *Thinking Photography*. Basingstoke: Macmillan.

Clark, Malcolm. 2000. "Benetton on Death Row." *New Statesman*, 24.1.2000.

Coles, Alex and Alexia Defert (eds). 2000. *de-, dis-, ex-. Interdisciplinarity: Art, Architecture, Theory*, Vol. 2. London: Black Dog Publishing.

Curran, James and Michael Gurevitch (eds). 2000. *Mass Media and Society*. London: Arnold.

Debord, Guy. 1967. *Society of the Spectacle*. Black and Red.

Eldridge, John, Jenny Kitzinger and Kevin Williams. 1997. *The Mass Media Power in Modern Britain*. Oxford: Oxford University Press.

Evans, Jessica (ed.). 1997. *The Camerawork Essays: Context and Meaning in Photography*. London: Rivers Oram.

Evans, Jessica and Stuart Hall. (eds). 1999. *Visual Culture: The Reader*, Thousand Oaks, CA and New Delhi: Sage and London: Open University.

Ewen, Stuart. 1976. *Captains of Consciousness: Advertising and the Social Roots of Consumer Culture*. New York: McGraw Hill.

Fielding, Helen. 1992. "Pulling the Woollies over Our Eyes: Benetton Advertising." *The Sunday Times*, 26.1.1992.

Hirsch, Marianne. 1997. *Family Frames: Photography, Narrative and Postmemory*. Cambridge, MA: Harvard University Press.

Lacan, Jacques. 1975. *The Seminars of Jacques Lacan, Book 1*. Cambridge: Cambridge University Press.

——. 1977. *Ecrits: A Selection*, trans. Alan Sheridan. New York: Norton.

Lee, Martin J. 2000. *The Consumer Society Reader*. Oxford: Blackwell.

Mantle, Jonathan. 1999. *Benetton: The Family, the Business and the Brand*. Great Britain: Warner Books.

Morley, David. 1992. *Television Audiences and Cultural Studies*. London: Routledge.

Mulvey, Laura. 1975. "Visual Pleasure and Narrative Cinema." *Screen* 16:3 (Autumn).

Murray, P. 1978. *The Penguin Dictionary of Art and Artists.* London: Penguin.

Myers, Kathy. 1986. *Understains: The Sense and Seduction of Advertising.* London: Comedia.

Nairne, Sandy. 1987. *State of the Art: Ideas and Images in the 1980s.* London: Chatto & Windus.

Powe, Lucas A. 1991. The Fourth Estate and the Constitution. Berkeley: University of California Press.

Rabinow, P. (ed.). 1984. *The Foucault Reader.* London: Peregrine.

Russell, F. 1993. *Colour Schemes, Arena* (June).

Solomon-Godeau, Abigail. 1991. *Photography in the Dock.* Minneapolis, MN: University of Minnesota Press.

Sparrow, Bartholomew H. 1999. *Uncertain Guardians: The News Media as a Political Institution.* Baltimore, MD and London: The Johns Hopkins University Press.

Stallybrass, P. and A. White. 1986. *The Politics and Poetics of Transgression.* London: Methuen.

Taylor, John. 1998. *Body Horror: Photojournalism, Catastrophe and War.* Manchester: Manchester University Press.

Watney, Simon. 1987. "Photography and Aids", *Ten 8*, No. 26.

White, C. 1992. "Blood, Sweaters and Designer Tears." *The Sunday Times*, 16.2.1992.

Willemen, Paul. 1978. "Notes on Subjectivity," *Screen* 19(1).

Williams, Raymond. 1965. *The Long Revolution.* Harmondsworth: Penguin.

Williamson, Judith. 1982. *Decoding Advertisements.* London: Marion Boyars.

Fashion Theory, Volume 6, Issue 1, pp. 111–114
Reprints available directly from the Publishers.
Photocopying permitted by licence only.
© 2002 Berg. Printed in the United Kingdom.

Exhibition Review:
Imperfect Beauty: The Making of Contemporary Fashion Photographs

**Reviewed by
Alistair O'Neill**

Alistair O'Neill teaches on the
new BA(Hons) Fashion
Photography Course at the
London College of Fashion.

**An exhibition at the Victoria and Albert Museum,
London, 28 September 2000–18 March 2001**

Imperfect Beauty ran at the same time and in the same gallery of the
museum as a thematic photographic exhibition titled *Attitude: A History
of Posing*. Picking up the combined gallery guide I couldn't help my eye
drifting towards a quotation by Diane Arbus advertising the other show:
*"You see someone on the street and essentially what you notice about
them is the flaw."* When this was seen in relation to the quotations that
were advertising *Imperfect Beauty* (*"I didn't care if the clothes were
creased—I wanted them to look as if a person owned them . . ."* etc.) it

became apparent that we weren't only to be concerned with artifice rather than reality, but also with making rather than seeing.

The curatorial intention was to get *"behind the surface gloss of fashion photography," "by focussing on the work behind the scenes."* With end-product eschewed, it was clearly stated that: *"Most of the material that you will see in this exhibition is the by-product of the working processes of photographers, stylists, art directors and hair and make-up artists . . ."* As the word *by-product* suggests, many of the exhibits were incidental and secondary; the notion of making furthered by a resistance to polish, in hopeful mimesis of the cultivated style of fashion photography that it sought to document and contextualize.

Any sense of *realness* that these practitioners are so keen to be judged by was swiftly eluded by a contrived recreation of influences for constructed images whose moments had long since passed. The somber quality of these posthumous lamentations (some people in the fashion industry call them *mood boards*) was taken to its conclusion by Corinne Day, who took the opportunity to exhibit the clothes of a dead friend.

From the manner of the displays it was clear that *Imperfect Beauty* was not so much expressed by the work but by the means of presentation. On casting an eye over the exhibits, irritation began with the odd glib assertion (*"Hairdressers don't travel light"*) or, for example, the inclusion of a badly drawn sketch of a mascara-laden eye. Pausing at a text label fashioned from a manila parcel label trimmed with a black lace frill, I pondered not only what was being communicated, but who agreed to its being communicated in this way? I longed for the curatorial equivalent of a bulldog clip to clamp the loosely tailored form of the idea more closely to the body of work in consideration.

Figure 1
Photographer: Elaine Constantine. Stylist: Polly Banks. Models: Victoria Brown, Michelle Moraal and Sarah Atkinson. The *Face*, December 1997.

Figure 2
Photographer: Corinne Day.
Stylist: Melanie Ward. "Rose
Brewer Street", 1993.

Even given that an idea of *fitting* is actively rejected by some of these practitioners, the resultant displays often managed to work to their detriment: a number of subtly resistant fashion photographs by David Sims were complemented by a clear-cut grammatical diagram of the fashion shoot as a fantasy football team by the photographer (Sims mid-field, his agent goalkeeper). Codifications and deconstructions further abounded; but by these demonstrations process was imbued with the same degree of self-consciousness as the very final image the exhibition was trying to resist.

I was reminded of a similar discrepancy in the filming of *The Eyes of Laura Mars*, the Hollywood film about a fashion photographer who has the ability to foresee murders. Helmut Newton is credited as photographic consultant to the film, and supplied his photographs for use as props in the film; yet in a scene depicting a studio fashion shoot, instead of shooting the models still—as is Newton's technique, the film has Laura Mars photographing them dancing. For the purpose of popular entertainment and for the medium of moving image, a degree of embellishment on working practice was necessary, as the process didn't sustain visual interest—it didn't keep the eye moving.

The necessity of embellishment to keep the eye moving is also to be found in Huysmans' nineteenth-century novel *Against Nature*, where the aesthete Des Esseintes has the shell of his tortoise gilded and bejeweled in order to satisfy his eye when it slowly moves across his oriental carpet. Returning from the jeweler to be placed on the carpet the tortoise dies, not from the weight of the embellishment but from the act of embellishing the shell.

These two examples serve to illustrate embellishment as both an act of beautifying and an act of fictitious additions. The former example falsifies process, the latter ruins by process. The problem with *Imperfect Beauty* as an aesthetic concept and as a record of creative practice as documented in this exhibition is not the flaw that Arbus believed you immediately notice in the subject, but in the subjective interpretation of its photographic record. A case of artifice embellishing reality, making embellishing seeing.

Notes for Contributors

Articles should be approximately 25 pages in length and *must* include a three-sentence biography of the author(s). Interviews should not exceed 15 pages and do not require an author biography. Film, exhibition and book reviews are normally 500 to 1,000 words in length. The Publishers will require a disk as well as a hard copy of any contributions (please mark clearly on the disk what word-processing program has been used). Berg accepts most programs with the exception of Clarisworks.

Fashion Theory: The Journal of Dress, Body & Culture will produce one issue a year devoted to a single topic. Persons wishing to organize a topical issue are invited to submit a proposal which contains a hundred-word description of the topic together with a list of potential contributors and paper subjects. Proposals are accepted only after review by the journal editor and in-house editorial staff at Berg Publishers.

Manuscripts
Manuscripts should be submitted to: *Fashion Theory: The Journal of Dress, Body & Culture*. Manuscripts will be acknowledged by the editor and entered into the review process discussed below. Manuscripts without illustrations will not be returned unless the author provides a self-addressed stamped envelope. Submission of a manuscript to the journal will be taken to imply that it is not being considered elsewhere for publication, and that if accepted for publication, it will not be published elsewhere, in the same form, in any language, without the consent of the editor and publisher. It is a condition of acceptance by the editor of a manuscript for publication that the publishers automatically acquire the copyright of the published article throughout the world. *Fashion Theory: The Journal of Dress, Body & Culture* does not pay authors for their manuscripts nor does it provide retyping, drawing, or mounting of illustrations.

Style
U.S. spelling and mechanicals are to be used. Authors are advised to consult *The Chicago Manual of Style (14th Edition)* as a guideline for style. *Webster's Dictionary* is our arbiter of spelling. We encourage the use of major subheadings and, where appropriate, second-level subheadings. Manuscripts submitted for consideration as an article must contain: a title page with the full title of the article, the author(s) name and address, and a three-sentence biography for each author. Do not place the author's name on any other page of the manuscript.

Manuscript Preparation
Manuscripts must be typed double-spaced (including quotations, notes, and references cited), one side only, with at least one-inch margins on standard paper using a typeface no smaller than 12pts. The original manuscript and a copy of the text on disk *(please ensure it is clearly marked with the word-processing program that has been used) must* be submitted, along with black and white *original* photographs (to be returned). Authors should retain a copy for their records. Any necessary artwork *must* be submitted with the manuscript.

Footnotes

Footnotes appear as 'Notes' at the end of articles. Authors are advised to include footnote material in the text whenever possible. Notes are to be numbered consecutively throughout the paper and are to be typed double-spaced at the end of the text. (Do not use any footnoting or end-noting programs which your software may offer as this text becomes irretrievably lost at the typesetting stage.)

References

The list of references should be limited to, and inclusive of, those publications actually cited in the text. References are to be cited in the body of the text in parentheses with author's last name, the year of original publication, and page number—e.g., (Rouch 1958: 45). Titles and publication information appear as 'References' at the end of the article and should be listed alphabetically by author and chronologically for each author. Names of journals and publications should appear in full. Film and video information appears as 'Filmography'. References cited should be typed double-spaced on a separate page. *References not presented in the style required will be returned to the author for revision.*

Tables

All tabular material should be part of a separately numbered series of 'Tables'. Each table must be typed on a separate sheet and identified by a short descriptive title. Footnotes for tables appear at the bottom of the table. Marginal notations on manuscripts should indicate approximately where tables are to appear.

Figures

All illustrative material (drawings, maps, diagrams, and photographs) should be designated 'Figures'. They must be submitted in a form suitable for publication without redrawing. Drawings should be carefully done with black ink on either hard, white, smooth-surfaced board or good quality tracing paper. Ordinarily, computer-generated drawings are not of publishable quality. Color photographs can be accepted but will be reproduced as black and white in the printed version of the journal. Whenever possible, photographs should be 8 x 10 inches. The publishers encourage artwork to be submitted as scanned files (300 dpi or above) on disk or via email. All figures should be clearly numbered on the back and numbered consecutively. All captions should be typed double-spaced on a separate page. Marginal notations on manuscripts should indicate approximately where figures are to appear. While the editors and publishers will use ordinary care in protecting all figures submitted, they cannot assume responsibility for their loss or damage. Authors are discouraged from submitting rare or non-replaceable materials. It is the author's responsibility to secure written copyright clearance on *all* photographs and drawings that are not in the public domain. Copyright should be obtained for worldwide rights and on-line publishing.

Criteria for Evaluation

Fashion Theory: The Journal of Dress, Body & Culture is a refereed journal. Manuscripts will be accepted only after review by both the editors and anonymous reviewers deemed competent to make professional judgments concerning the quality of the manuscript. Upon request, authors will receive reviewers' evaluations.

Reprints for Authors

Twenty-five reprints of authors' articles will be provided to the first named author free of charge. Additional reprints may be purchased upon request.